Acclaim for Danell Lynn's *Philanthropic Wanderlust*

"A nomad with a heart of gold, Danell transports the reader to the remote, poverty-stricken and at times dangerous regions of the world, allowing them to witness first-hand her missions of hope. You will be hooked from the first page as you accompany this courageous, unselfish, compassionate and adventurous young woman making the world a better place for those less fortunate. An uplifting read that will no doubt encourage others to unleash their own humanitarian journey..."

-Teresa Rodriguez – Bestselling author – *Daughters of Juarez*, Emmy-Award winning Journalist - Univision News Magazine Show *Aqui y Ahora*

"Danell Lynn is a remarkable woman with a remarkable story. Philanthropic Wanderlust introduces you to her journey of personal reinvention and discovering a purpose through adventurous travel. From brutality and kindness in the mountains of Central America to the kindling of hope from despair in the warm heart of Africa, Danell offers unflinching honesty and thought-provoking insight into the reality of life for the people touched by her compassion. Philanthropic Wanderlust will give you the gift of new perspective and a renewed faith in the power of one person to make a difference."

-Iain Harper, Executive Director - *Jupiter's Travellers*- *Ted Simon Foundation*

"I was kept focused by the world of opportunities that Danell has created and taken advantage of. She should be an inspiration to all."

-Sam Manicom, author of the
Adventure Motorcycle Travel Books

"...There is so much feeling in Danell's desire to not only travel the world, but be of significant value to it! It captures her spirit, her empathetic nature, her lust for life, and her most altruistic style."

-Allen Naille, retired CEO of Amfac Resorts Inc

"This book not only inspires a desire to serve others, but also creates awareness of how much others struggle throughout the world. This book is hard to put down after the first page because it literally feels like the journey is shared between the author and the reader."

-Lisa Aaroe, PhD

"...The true ability of a writer is an ability to take words and paint a picture in the readers mind and Danell has painted a masterpiece..."

- Brandon Green, Fire Fighter

"I loved the book...it brings to life many experiences ... in a wonderful way ...really enjoyed being vicariously pulled into the experiences I've not had and felt as if I was a part of her travels and travails. It's amazing the author does this all for charity."

-Jim Green USAF Retired
5th grade Teacher

Purposeful Wanderings

Young Readers Edition of Philanthropic Wanderlust

Written and Illustrated
By

DANELL LYNN, M.ED

ISBN-13: 978-1502363794
ISBN-10: 1502363798

Cover Art: Danell Lynn
Photos: Danell Lynn, unless otherwise indicate
Illustration: Danell Lynn
Typeface of choice Cambria, occasional Garamond & Lucida Calligraphy

Cover: Paintings credits-"Eyes Don't Lie" series by Danell Lynn Painting of a young Colombian child.

Printed in the United States of America

DEDICATION

To those that took the time to educate me, and to all those that give their hearts and passion to continue the education of our future. Thank you for believing in the power of young hearts...we do grow up and change the world – even if just a little corner of it!

Purposeful – having a clear aim or purpose.

Wanderings - a going about from place to place.

(as defined by Merriam-Webster dictionary)

"Remembrance of things past is not necessarily the remembrance of thing as they were."
– Marcel Proust

This book is written with the best memory that I can put on paper as I sit back with my journals and cup of coffee, manically attempting to meet my own personal deadline! As any two people hearing one speaker will interpret it in two different ways, this is my interpretation of my travels and experiences reflecting my perceptions of the world and cultures I have explored. A few minor details in this book, such as public agency names and personal names have remained, occasionally with use of first names only. From time to time names and dates have been changed completely to protect privacy, not all could be contacted. In some instances events have been compressed or time periods rearranged to better serve the narrative. At times names were simply memory blanks, I am much better with faces than names...I am working on it! It is written as a work of non-fiction, and is a true account of events; I have not knowingly misrepresented any parts of the journey.

But if you cannot laugh at yourself, what else is there, Happy reading.

-Danell Lynn

When a heart desires cultural exploration it is quite difficult to block out the pounding rhythms of wanderlust.

Purposeful Wanderings is the Young Reader edition of *Philanthropic Wanderlust,* in hopes to inspire new generations of humanitarian adventurers.

CONTENTS

Preface

PREFACE

"Nothing is impossible, the word itself says I'm possible." – Audrey Hepburn

I consider myself an explorer, although the explorations I read about in history class where the first flags were placed or the first anchors thrown to new lands is a stake I will never pound and a rope I will never throw. I still find great thrills in packing my bags for undiscovered lands in my personal past, a country unstamped in my passport is the stake of my exploration.

I am a cultural explorer, a global citizen. Through travel, humanitarian projects and a desire to keep experiencing the world is my passionate journey of exploration.

I have passed into my third decade of life,
I have been to over 40 countries, all 50 states of
my home country,
And have always felt at home on the road.

I have been called a wanderer, lost, adventurous,
brave, creative, crazy...

What do I classify myself as
...

Just simply...ME

Welcome to my philanthropic adventures in
wanderland

Indulge

We all have talents and differences that make life quite exciting, and the one truth is that you are the ONLY one that can be YOU, do so greatly.

When deciding what it is you have to give to fellow human beings, it can be grueling. I first found immense sadness in working through this process:

I am not a doctor
I can't save lives
...
I am not a millionaire
How can I make a difference...with so little
...
I am not an engineer
I can't invent amazing ways for fresh
Water or safe cooking
....
What can I do / give

This went on in my mind for a while then it hit me to allow in vulnerability. The willingness to open doors and walk through. I am an artist, an educator, a writer, a designer, a traveler, - could this all come together to make something great?

YES!

Thus what I have to give was given birth.

It started extremely small with the first trip to El

Salvador and a backpack with a box of Crayola's (64 crayon set), set of 20 markers, 1 ream of blank computer paper, and a packet of lined paper (100 sheets).

Thus the birth of Highwire, a company dedicated to bringing art to children and helping to bridge the cultural gaps through arts education.

How much can youth do? There are school and homework and afterschool extracurricular activities - can they blend together?

YES!

No need to just focus on one thing, or in one direction. One does not need to create a company to find ways to make a difference in the lives of others. In today's culture knowledge is literally at our fingertips. Want to know what youth are doing to change the world, causes they support, or where to donate items you have collected simply type it into a search engine on the internet.

I learned early on not to limit my life to one dream, I can achieve all my dreams, except maybe the idea that I once had to be a lead singer in a band. My voice, well not even really award winning for shower singing so I had to pass up on that dream.

*   *   *

At the time that Highwire and Threading Hope* began I was living in an artist residence, a community facility of low-income housing. I had life changing circumstances and left my job with only $345 in savings. I moved to the artist residence and took the time to fall in love with ME, with life, and what I wanted from it. During my 18-months stay I realized how important giving was to me, and thus with pick up jobs here and there. While living at well below the poverty line, I launched humanitarian companies that would focus on children and families in need. I wanted to rebuild my life the exact way I dreamed it would be. I started and launched dl-couture a high end clothing company (still running), built up my existing art company Dl Fine Artist, both of which would be the launching companies as humanitarian organizations. Dl-couture would have Threading Hope, and Dl Fine Artist would launch Highwire. The stories of launching high end fashion and art companies while making ten dollars an hour scrubbing toilets at a local motel is a book in itself, but both were launched with a foundation in giving, in releasing my philanthropic spirit that so badly needed out!

*Find more about both of these humanitarian entities in Appendix B

Finding your passion and celebrating it will always fill you with joy. Giving of yourself to others around the world and letting the engulfing spirit of happiness and smiles that you helped create, become a part of you - that is philanthropy. I choose to create mine with the funds that I have, I don't do fundraisers and am not a 501c3. I try to create businesses that will fund them (like HumaniHandbags.com, a 50% profit share fashion-forward company, 10% from dl-couture sales, portion of book sales and my continued salary from working in the state education system).

Highwire was born with one box of crayons, some papers and the smiles of displaced children. It only took one trip and the joys that art lesson created for orphans of Soyapango sparked the flame that will forever burn. Stretching a wire across borders, bridging the cultural gaps through arts, as of 2014 Highwire has provided art lessons and backpacks full of art kits to over 180 children in more than six countries and three continents.

Threading Hope came out of a discussion about a young man coming to the United States for reconstructive surgery, a new idea began to take shape. The young man was 12- years old and burned on over 80% of his body when an oven exploded. My mom attended the VIP event with me and when she heard of his story said, "Wouldn't it be great if we could do something to comfort him; I think I want to make him a quilt for recovery in the hospital." It was in this moment that moved my mother's heart that we launched Threading Hope to bring comfort and warmth to many around the world through handmade quilts. By 2014 we had reached over 130 families, from six countries, and continue to collect donations of quilts from quilt groups, schools and individuals that want to share in our philanthropic movement.

Life has stages and brick roads that are anything but yellow, and my advice is never, never take the yellow brick road...create your own path of adventure and let the windows and doors open to a life that you never knew existed. Step through the fear of uncertainty and embrace it with love!

You never know the excitement that life will hold for you, even when you think you have it planned life will remind you to take on another challenge.

"Life is either a daring adventure or nothing."
–Helen Keller

Good Eats: pupusas - cornmeal pocket filled w/cheeze

REPUBLICA DE
EL SALVADOR, C.A.
TARJETA DE TURISMO
TOURIST CARD

No. 21229

$10.00
TEN. U.S. DOLLARS

APELLIDOS (LAST NAMES): Danell Lynn
NOMBRES (GIVEN NAMES): American
NACIONALIDAD (NATIONALITY): 981188
PASAPORTE (PASSPORT No.):
LUGAR Y PROCEDENCIA (ARRIVING FROM):
ESTADIA OTORGADA (AUTHORIZED STAY): 60

PROHIBIDO REALIZAR TRABAJO REMUNERADO
GAINFULL EMPLOYMENT PROHIBITED

OCAM
A100K/110n 60

EL SALVADOR

⊕ SAN
Salvador

capital: San Salvador
language: Spanish

CHAPTER
ONE

Philanthropy and the First Lady

This was the beginning of a trip that almost ended it all. Danell Lynn's heart sank. After having been pick-pocketed, witness to gang violence and exposed to road casualties all she wanted was to go home. The plane never arrived.

But this was not where it all began. It began with a backpack, a ream of paper, a box of crayons, and a dream for global art lessons for children – bridging the cultural gaps through art.

Looking back into the first five years it is inspiring how big a small goal has become. In 2007 Danell created her fashion and art companies with giving in mind. Soon after she created her **humanitarian** companies *Threading Hope* and *Highwire*. Even just two years prior (in 2005) Danell never imagined creating such companies nor watching them grow to the extent that occurs each year. Every year more and more children are part of bridging global cultural gaps with the art kits and lessons of *Highwire* and more and more families are comforted with handmade quilts of *Threading Hope*.

*   *   *

<u>Day One</u>

The air was thick and filled with lush smells of fresh flowers in bloom. As Danell walked out of the airport a light breeze wrapped around her like a soothing hug for a welcome to El Salvador. She had been invited on this trip as a guest of another charity organization to **volunteer** with their program and to launch *Highw*ire.

Donated boxes of food, clothing, shoes, toys and more where waiting at the airport. All the volunteers grabbed some boxes and loaded the vans, then they were off headed to the Magnolia Hotel for a late breakfast.

Now one thing can be said about food and Danell – she loves to eat! Whether in a **foreign** land or at home her enjoyment of food is clear. Her first meal in El Salvador consisted of refried black beans, eggs, and toast. A meal she quickly learned to love- the creaminess of the blended rich black beans filled the empty pit in her stomach. After breakfast and a quick check-in to the hotel rooms the group was off for the first round of donation deliveries.

The first stop was Kiwanis Village – "Chatterera"- where once was a wasteland of trash disposal now set rows of homes. After a large earthquake many homes were destroyed and this trash heap got a makeover to create new homes for the victims of the **natural disaster**.

As the van pulled into the village Danell was one of the first volunteers out the door and swarms of children surrounded her. Little hands reached up and grabbed at her arms and neck. She was pulled to her knees! It could have been scary if it were not the perfect level for tiny hugs and gentle cheek kisses. The air became filled with the sounds of childhood laughter and smiles were abundant.

The real excitement began as the boxes were opened and food and toys were given out. It did not take long for the excitement to turn into mild chaos as the soccer balls were thrown into the crowds of children.

After all donations were given out the group walked through the village. The homes were made from corrugated tin and wooden pallets. Items discarded as trash in the US were used to create homes and provide shelter and comfort to many families here.

Day Two

A not so typical welcome to school

In Soyapango, San Salvador the team was greeted by smiling children in perfectly pressed uniforms and men with machine guns and pistols. The armed guards were likely due to the presence of the First Lady Mrs. Saca of El Salvador. Danell would also find out days later that this was one of the most unsafe cities in El Salvador, thus the need for the armed guards.

Although guards walking the streets and guarding public buildings is not common in the US in much of the developing world this can be a common site. None the less the group made their way through the gates and were seated for a presentation by El Salvadorian government officials (including the First Lady) to thank them for the kind work done in this country. As headsets were passed around Danell felt a bit of relief as translation would come right through the earphones so even with her minimal Spanish skills she would not miss a beat!

When the "Thank-You" concluded the **donations** were ready to begin and it was time for the first lesson of *Highwire*. Danell was allowed to count off 20 children and head over to an open air courtyard for the very first of this program. She had created a lesson called "*barefeet*" where the children would place their foot on blank paper, trace their foot with crayons and then fill the blank edges in with words or pictures of their hopes and dreams. All of the children wished for trees (árboles) and many a house (una casa), others for bicycletas, cats (gatos) and some even an ice-cream cone (helado). The children would point to their drawing and say the Spanish word and Danell would say the English word and then they would switch, each trying to speak the others language and teach each other.

As Danell continued to teach, she found herself observing a young boy about 12 years old. He was helping his younger brother of probably age 8 or 9 years with the lesson and through the line (una línea) to collect some art supplies. The older brother held him around the shoulders standing behind as a guide - this gentleness moved Danell. They were both **orphans** and the older brother had been taking care of his younger brother for a few years. The younger sibling had an intellectual disability and thus had more difficulty than the other children around him. There was no teasing present and the companionship of his elder brother mimicked more of a protector than sibling.

As class was coming to an end a few of the children gave Danell big hugs and wanted her to have their art work. Even with the minimal grasp of the language much came back to her as she ran the lessons and communicated with the children with no translator. It was inspiring in more ways than one, and she knew at that moment, what she had to give and share with the world!

After the completion of the art lesson she went back up to the main courtyard to help with giving out the donations. In the chaos of the deliveries, lines had broken up and crowds pushed through to the boxes. It was a mad rush of people pushing and scrambling to get more than the ration they were allotted. At some time during this **chaos**, while being grabbed and bumped constantly, Danell's back pocket was unbuttoned and her camera pick-pocketed. The fact that she was robbed in a school on a humanitarian mission made her sad, but what saddened her most was the loss of the photos from the past two days. She was surprised when tears came; it was not her first travel experience, and not her first loss, but the tears came anyway.

To her surprise as well, she was treated rudely by some leading members of the charity foundation stating, "*You must have lost or misplaced it; they don't steal here!*" This greatly hurt her heart she was not prepared to be called, pretty much, a liar by other "humanitarians" on this trip. The only rational explanation she could think to justified to herself was maybe there was worry if she said it was stolen it would affect future trips or donors to that foundation. She still does not know why she was treated this way, and it bothered her more than the actual theft. Sometimes people can be cruel and although we may wish to understand why – we may never know where hateful words or actions come from.

Ironically the one who gave Danell the greatest respect over the situation and apologized was the First Lady, Mrs. Saca. She received word of what occurred and treated Danell with honest knowledge of what can take place in rough areas, even when trying to do good. She sent her assistant to the hotel to speak with Danell that night. They asked Danell to create a letter to have on file of the theft. In composing the letter together indicating what had occurred it was mandated by the government staff that she write in the letter the word "mugging" although in the US it would be called "pick-pocketing / robbed" -

a mugging to Danell would be more extreme and she would have bruises, but this was the word that must be written. After they created a timeline and noted the type of camera that had been stolen. She was told it would be replaced, and already feeling downhearted, she did not hold her breath. That same day, Lillislot, the First Lady's go-to-gal, brought photos that had been taken at the school earlier during the project. It was a great honor for Danell to receive a photo of Mrs. Saca that was signed by her with Thank you's for the work that had been done.

Thus began *Highwire*. Danell would not let a little negative incident bring the dream down! The bounce back began. A few months later she was gladly proven wrong when a new camera from El Salvador, a Cannon Powershot with Spanish settings, arrived at her doorstep. It was not just the camera, but rather the honesty of the First Lady that moved her. Danell's belief in humanity had slowly been returning and this bumped it into rapid speed. It is easy when let down, or broken hearted to lose faith in fellow human beings. But as the days click by something will occur that rejuvenates your belief in people, and the human race once again becomes a collage of cultures with all pieces offering something new to learn.

Life's a Beach

It was a quick two days of deliveries and art. As the group of charity foundation members got ready to head back to the US Danell was trying to decide if she should stay for the extra days. She had originally extended her plane ticket for two more days but should she head home early. She was still feeling a bit upset with the way she was treated and was not sure if she was up to solo travel to other parts of the country. She decided to sleep on it and see how she felt in the morning. Getting up early she headed to the café for breakfast and talked with two members of the group that also decided to stay, Mike S. and Mike D, they both had extended their tickets an extra couple days to see more of the country.

Over coffee they decided that none of them just wanted to sit at the current location so they threw around some ideas and within 15 minutes a plan was made. They would head to the beach town of El Zonte for some sun, swimming, surfing and laying around time in **hammocks.**

Once they arrived they found an amazing hotel right on the beach for just $45.00 split 3 ways. Not a bad deal at all for a unit with air conditioning, rooftop dining and a view that over looked the breaking waves of the ocean.   After a long ride to get here they were all excited to jump right into the ocean and get a little surfing in! But alas the signs were up for a dangerous **undertow** and no swimming was allowed. Feeling a bit odd with the ocean was in view, they jumped into the safe, calm, swimming pool and gazed at the beautiful ocean. After a quick dip they then went for a beach walk and noticed picnic tables that were unusually busy.

As they got closer they noticed the line of families and children waiting for what were on the tables - boxes of medicine and goods. Here under an awning, on simple picnic tables had become an **impromptu** medical clinic. Talking with the local group at the clinic they learned it occurs once a month and gets **vaccines,** books, clothes, and more to the children and families of the smaller mountain villages that cannot make it into the city for medical services.   Danell could not believe this only happens once a month and they happened to be here on the day it occurred, she was feeling like it was a sign that she was on the right path to leading a more humanitarian centered life.

They then walked on into the village to *La Casa De Frieda* for dinner, a spot they had learned about from the locals.   Danell excitedly ordered her new El Salvadorian favorite meal the eggs and beans, huevos y frijoles negros – she exclaimed, "so good!"

As she ate Danell began to talk with the owner of the restaurant and learned that she had attended college in the United States on **scholarship** and even had a doctorate! The owner always dreamed of running a restaurant although she did state it was quite hard to find local workers because many of them have families in the US. The locals' family that ventured to the US (legally or illegally) would send back their earnings and it was enough money each month that their family in El Salvador did not need to work. As they continued to talk of the business difficulties they chewed on coffee beans from the local farm which added another layer of cultural experience in getting to know the area and the traditions.

On the walk back to their hotel the trio saw a sign for a van driver that goes to Guatemala from El Zonte. It would mean traveling into another country, which was quite exciting for Danell - she did not take long to decided it was a great idea! They booked the van for the next morning because staying put here they could not do much in the small beach town with a closed – dangerous ocean. They packed that night for the early morning, 5:30 am departure time was quickly approaching.

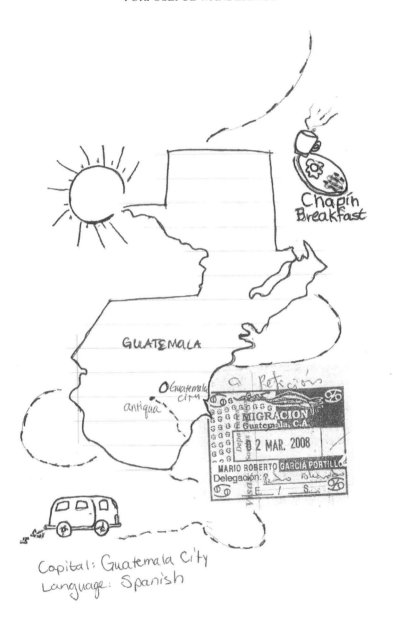

Chapín
Breakfast

GUATEMALA

○Guatemala
city

antigua

a Petén

MIGRACION
Guatemala, C.A.

0 2 MAR. 2008

MARIO ROBERTO GARCIA PORTILLO
Delegación:

E / S.

Capital: Guatemala City
Language: Spanish

CHAPTER
THREE

Fated to be Darkly Memorable

It was an early start and as they woke up Mike S. decided he wanted to stay and work with the local groups providing vaccines. He said, "I know they needed my fee," so he did not ask for a refund and just gave up his money so Danell and Mike D. could carry on. It was **honorable** because if the van did not take three people it would cancel the trip – due mostly in part to fuel cost. So Mike D. and Danell packed up and were off for the four hour ride to Antigua, Guatemala.

Danell had fallen in and out of sleep lulled by the mountain roads with gentle curves and inclines, then a sudden STOP! The police had one side of the road closed off and as the van crept closer it was clear why there was such a sudden stop. Through the large windows two bodies could be seen lying on the road, they were clearly deceased. One was being zipped up into a medical bag, yet the other lay uncovered on the asphalt. When the view goes from beautiful mountain roads to the scene that was in front of them, it took a bit to register just what had occurred. The van guide, Martin, told the group that this was due to gang violence and that they were just left here on the road as a statement. He said he could tell from the pants one of the young men wore that he was affiliated with a gang. He explained that violence increases during political elections and that occasionally a political point is made with death, utilizing the local gangs to deliver the message.

It was a very real reminder of how different cultures approach death, and also a reminder of how quickly life can change. The trip to this point had been filled with highlights and deep lows, Danell found herself wondering what she was doing here. It had only been three days and she had been pick-pocketed, treated rudely and now was witness to gang violence in the wide open space between El Salvador and Guatemala.

When they arrived in Antigua it was beautiful. **Cobblestone** streets lined with aged buildings and markets filled with color. It was a much need rejuvenation. They dropped their bags at El Gato Negro (the Black Cat) Inn, and then it was lunch time. When Martin came back Mike D. had decided that he just wanted to have a massage and rest, and Danell could not understand to come this far and not experience the city –and they only had one day! Well Martin would not let Danell travel the city alone so he joined her for the day as a personal tour guide, he did not charge her, he just wanted to show her his city!

The first stop was the Sky Café for grilled cheese and really good café con leche. (Coffee and milk) When traveling often locals open their hearts to share their cities and culture and it usually ends up being a wonderfully unique experience. The open air deck of this eatery overlooked the entire city. They chatted about experiences in their home counties, enjoyed the rolling clouds coming down the hills and just took in all the city had to offer. A stunning elegance surrounded them with volcanoes, historic buildings, and below on the city streets people began to **bustle**. In their conversations over coffee Danell had told Martin about the ordeal with her camera, and he offered to let her borrow his camera for the day and then he would download the pictures to a cd before she left. She felt very lucky as a couple people from the charity in El Salvador shared their photos from the first two days, and now Martin was offering his camera for her to capture Guatemalan memories.

They went to art museums, walked the charming streets and then to the historic San Francisco Church. It reminded Danell of European castle ruins she had visited as a teenager while living in England. This church was destroyed by floods and mudslides in the 1700's. The old rock walls and formations throughout the grounds were a reminder to Danell how truly young she really is.

The reconstruction of the main cathedral was stunning, and most of the original work was ruins but worth a walk through. Occasionally you could get a glimpse through the windows of the coffee bean plants flanked on either side. The tomb of Santo Hermano Pedro de San Jose de Betancurt was here, housed in the private chapel for worship. Many still come to pray to him and show gratitude for his work with the poor. His is known for his healing and giving that has been carried through stories from generation to generation for thousands of years.

When you only get one day in a city, you pack it in...well at least that is how Danell travels. She wanted the most from her time, and Martin was completely on board. They took off running but left time for lunch of course! It was the best food yet! Martin ordered as he knew this local place well, and with Danell being a vegetarian-she decided to trust instead of work **diligently** at translating the menu. What she got was amazing, a large plate that they both could eat from filled with cooked veggies and bean curd shish kabobs with rice. It was a palate **invigorating** meal.

Travel is unique and often you get surprised. There was a **procession** walking through the city streets on this one day out of the year that they were in Guatemala and they got to see it all. The locals participating in the procession walked the streets dressed in long deep purple robes with tall pointed hats. There was the smell of incense, balanced by the sounds of music as people sang and chanted. Echoes bounced off old stone walls filling your heart with the traditions and years of worship that surround Antigua's history.

There are a lot of expats and travelers in Antigua. At evening's end, Martin invited the group to his house for pizza and a gathering of many travelers including his American girlfriend. It was a melting pot of cultures, breaking bread or chowing down pizza. There were Germans, English, and four Americans (two from Colorado,

one from New York and one from Washington).
They talked about many subjects and often the
topic of conversation was the world watching the
US waiting for its economy to collapse. (It was
2008 when the USA was experiencing a financial
crash with the world was taking notice).
Conversations did not stay heavy for long, as
they filled their bellies with pizzas and then
laughter began to fill the tall ceilings. It was a
great end to a wonderful day.

The next morning was another early to rise day
as they had to cross the borders to catch their
flights home. As they got back into El Salvador it
seemed fated that this trip would be darkly
memorable...another dead body. This time very
close, right on the edge of the road. A man was
hit right after a tight curve as the road turned.
He must have been hit by a large vehicle and it
appeared that it kept on driving. On the edge of
the road in the bushes sat a woman in **hysterics**.
Danell assumed this was his wife, as the pain
from her screams could only be that of a loved
one. It was different here; there was not a rush
to clean the scene or cover bodies. The police
were there but just stood in conversation. It was
at this pivotal point in life that Danell learned she
looked at the world, and death a little differently.
Mike D. looked at her with tears in his eyes and
asked judgmentally, "Why are you not crying,
does it not affect you?" She felt taken aback by
this, as yes it affected her but obviously not in
the same way it did him. She got quiet and

finished the ride to the airport in silence. *"I wondered to myself if I lacked a connection that my fellow human beings had, or was my view more of an* **anthropological** *view and distanced as an observer?"*

An element of travel that follows you no matter where you go-is you have to get to your destination as well as getting home. Whether by plane, train, or overland adventure vehicle, there is still a circular element that brings you back to where you started. Bags were checked and all passengers waited, and they waited. Then they learned the plane never left Miami and there was only one flight a day...so they were delayed - stuck in El Salvador! Danell felt her heart sink a little, having been mugged-pick-pocketed, and the combined emotions resulting from the treatment surrounding the camera theft, the gang violence of two bodies, and the road casualty of one body. Danell never wanted so badly to go home. She was given a taxi pass but was hesitant as locals had told her travel was unsafe for single females at night and a hotel voucher for a room that was a 40-minute drive away was a long solo taxi ride. She found herself exhausted standing at the edge of the gate, and staring out at nothingness, expecting to just wake up from it all.

Mugging, death and a hopeful heart

As she stared out into nothingness, suddenly there was a hand on her shoulder. An elegant woman asked, "Are you alone? Are you planning to take a taxi alone?" Danell **stammered** a "yyyy-yes" and was told "absolutely unacceptable" and that she would be accompanying her and her driver to the hotel. The woman told Danell that "it is unsafe to travel in a taxi alone." They waited for her driver and got to know each other a little better.

About six years prior to this trip while attending an art college Danell was living in Miami, Florida and days like today reminded her how small the world truly is. Many of those on the cancelled flight were in El Salvador for a very "to-do" wedding, a "who's-who's" of Miami, all with ties to El Salvador. It was a lovely blend of her past life in Miami, reconnecting here in El Salvador.

Life can take you on some pretty amazing roads and not all paths are marked.

Maria E. Cosculluela, was the Vice-President of an interior design company in Miami (Coral Gables). She was the generous soul that provided Danell the private car ride to her hotel. She introduced Danell to Teresa Rodriguez – television anchor for Univision Network and host of the program "Aqui y Ahora" a news magazine show, translated into "Here and Now". Teresa is an award winning journalist, author, and more. They all three began to chat about Danell's work in El Salvador, her experiences and a book she was working on at the time about the border issues of Arizona and Mexico. A book that took a tri-cultural perspective surrounding the "border issue." Teresa told Danell of her book, *Daughters of Juarez,* a true labor of love of investigative journalism concerning the serial murders south of the border. (Months later Danell opened her mailbox to a lovely surprise; she had been sent an autographed copy and in it was encouraged to continue her work and her writing). In talking with these strong and motivated women, there were discussions about being women, **entrepreneurs** as well as **humanitarians**. The discussion started to lighten Danell's mood and open her eyes to the thought that maybe her flight was cancelled because she had not learned or experienced what she was supposed to in El Salvador.

They parted with hugs and exchanged information as they dropped Danell off at her hotel, Teresa and Maria were staying a different hotel. It had been a few hours of wondrous conversation with two great women, who both are very driven and take part in many ventures. It is always an inspiration to meet others dedicated to fully living and giving all they have to this short existence we call LIFE.

As Danell waited in line to check-in to her room for the night her stomach let her know of the delay in eating. It was then that she met Mario Cader-French in line awaiting room assignments. He is an El Salvadorian who lived in Miami where he was the Vice President of Public Affairs for the MTV Networks Latin America. Danell later learned of his many other **endeavors** and his philanthropic nature. Just as the amazing women Danell had met earlier, he too had created and developed many programs and raised awareness of many important issues. They chatted and re-hashed Danell's time and experiences in country... He said, "Unacceptable, you will come to dinner tonight with my family and I to find the true El Salvadorian experience." The offer was generous and they agreed to go to their rooms to dress for dinner and meet in the lobby an hour later.

His family dinner included his immediate and extended family from siblings to aunts and uncles. It was a truly beautiful experience with ten plus people gathered around a large table. It was here when Mario began to tell of Danell's experience that his sister gasped and stated that she had lived here her entire life and had never seen a dead body. She could not believe that Danell had seen three in just four days. Those at the table could not ingest all the "experience" that Danell had gained in less than a week in country. They began to open their hearts and tell her vivid stories of their childhoods and the beauty that is El Salvador. They laughed as she told them she was in Soyapango. They never go there. They questioned why she had ventured to the "most unsafe city in El Salvador"... they all laughed.

During dinner she was introduced to Rafael Diaz, an artist, and discussed paintings, art, his work and hers, as they filled their mouths with utterly delicious food! Mario's family was very involved in El Salvador and meeting them was the gem for Danell from her trip. She also met Michel, Marios's uncle who creates museums and has art dating back to historical periods, modern and even an old **Andy Warhol** that he just keeps in his closet. He said he did not know where to hang it....an original Andy Warhol in the closet... one could only laugh! This entire family had known Danell for only hours yet opened up and accepted her as one of their own. The conversations and laughter filled the restaurant, and the smiles and sparkle in their faces warmed her soul. Her experience of El Salvador began to morph. She no longer felt the depressing need to flee. She would leave on her morning flight lighter and knowing that her humanitarian path was the right road to be on.

Fate stepped in at a time of need and let Danell see the light through the cloud that was hovering over her. The plane needed to be canceled, as it was the only way to address her negative emotions from this trip and truly do a 180 after meeting such amazing people. Danell returned home to tell stories that did not just include the dark or sad aspects of her trip but also the humorous side-notes and the wonderful conversations of people she had met and the family that took her in as their own! El Salvador has a special place in her heart, as do its people.

Because of all the amazing individuals that got bumped due to a flight delay…Danell now looks at flight mishaps and delays in an entirely new way - as a life lesson. Her future will hold more flight delays, yet none as moving as her extended time in San Salvador, at least not yet.

Capital: Rabat
Official Languages
Arabic

Rabat
CasaBlanca
Morocco
algeria
WESTERN SAHARA
Mauritania

Good eats: seKsu
(Couscous w/vegi's
Heaps of Meat for
enjoyers of Flesh)

CHAPTER
FIVE

Air of Wanderlust
Paris → Casablanca

A large part of the wanderlust spirit is the wandering path to get where you are going, Tucson to Atlanta – Atlanta to Paris- Paris to Casablanca, the last leg of the journey just exuded a bit of romance... a flight from Paris to Casablanca!

This trip carried an air of courtship that differed from other adventures. This foray was a go-see for *Threading Hope* and *Highwire*, and a cataloging of stories and events. Danell was traveling with three other women, one of whom, Leah, was a lawyer investigating the violation of human rights (of which Danell was invited to be a part of some very deep and expressive interviews). Another woman Nancy Huff, who runs *Teach the Children International*, and Lynn, who works in conflict resolution. Danell would meet with locals that ran orphanages, women entrepreneurship foundations, and so much more. In meeting with the King's Council she learned of where she might be of service with the youth in conjunction with government agencies. Danell was able to see how *Threading Hope* and *Highwire* could help and support humanitarian goals they have.

This was a suit and tie style trip and upon arrival in Casablanca they were picked up and escorted to the VIP lounge. They enjoyed warm mint and green tea as government officials took their passports through customs. They were simply told to sit back and relax... into the leather sofas; sip some tea from ornately decorated glasses and a silver tea pot, "*oh, only if I must!*"

The car was ready outside with the door held open as Danell gently glided into the beautiful black Audi that would deliver them to their meetings. No bus routes to navigate, no walking for hours to get where needed, just roll out of bed, get dressed and meet the car! One could get used to this.

Casablanca to Laâyoune

They only had this morning and early afternoon in Casablanca before the flights to Laâyoune, and that's a lot of time if you travel the way Danell does- so off to Ricks Café. A must in Casablanca, and the food was tasty but the piano just kept calling her, she so badly wanted to sit and jam out a tune to the patrons. Then she remembered it had been over 12 years since her fingers had the pleasure of gliding over piano keys, thus Danell regressed to just the visual in her mind of rocking out at Ricks!

After an enjoyable meal at Rick's and getting to know the ladies better, there was still time for Hasann II Mosque, and it was magnificent. Upon arrival the fog laid low hugging to the bellowing waters. As they walked closer to the entrance, it began to clear and the vastness of the ocean became visible. On one side of the **minaret** was a brown hue, coated in dust and sea salts, and the other was pure white. The Great Mosque minaret is said to be the tallest structure in Morocco and the tallest minaret in the world, standing near 689 feet and at night shines a laser into the skies "pointing the way to God."

They arrived during the six year cycle of cleaning that is needed due to the erosion caused by the sea. Thus some of the ornately carved structures where shrouded in scaffolding but if you look closely you could still see the amazing work that occurred so many years ago.

Slipping off their shoes, they handed over tickets for the English tour and entered the breathtaking and ethereal archway. The walls reached to the sky with pure whiteness created with a specialty plaster mix that included egg whites, and the ceilings bring you back down with their dark woods, stained from spices and lined with gold leaf. At first glance one would never know that the roof can open like a football stadium. It was made for special occasions to open to the heavens, for instance, Ramadan Prayer when 20,000 people are in this Mosque and they need air so the roof opens.

The prayer hall was lined with a raised platform on the right side that housed the women. They were completely closed in with beautiful wooden carved patterned windows with just enough of a view that all one could see would be their eyes. Then the group ventured to the basement for the *Fountains of Ablution* where one washes before entering to pray. The **hammam** baths had its own entrance and used the Tadelakt plastering technique of egg white and black soap mixture accented by hand painted inset tiles for pops of color.

Today was a bit of touring; tomorrow the meetings would begin that would fill the week from Eco-Development organization and treatment plants visits, to hospitals, orphanages, a meeting with a woman's business organization, discussions with victims of human rights violations and more. Tonight after dinner, a private in-home visit to hear one woman's story of life decisions that were made for her and her family without choice.

*　　　*　　　*

It had been a full day from the morning in Morocco, the flights to the Western Sahara, an 8pm dinner, and an amazing opportunity at 2am for an in-home invitation to hear Sadani Malainine's journey. Moroccans, Danell quickly learned, stay very active into the night and early morning. At first she just thought sleep evaded them as her group would have meetings at 7 am and continue all the through the day and into the night. But some prefer the night and resting in the day while others work during daylight. Danell's group just had a good mix throughout their time here that they filled many hours of every day. It was exhausting and exhilarating.

Sadani Malainine invited them to her private home to tell them her story of her family and other families that were made to separated. But before the storytelling began the welcome ritual needed to occur.

They were welcomed into her home as family and enjoyed the three cups of tea and plates of handmade sweets. Each woman was offered a gift and honored to be wrapped in traditional fabric and tied into their new *melfas* for the evening or more accurately stated for the morning. Danell loved her gift; it was a beautiful white fabric with green sparkles throughout. She stood arms out in silence as Sadani wrapped the *melfas* around her body and tucked the long length of fabric back into itself at the waist creating a full head to toe covering that just left your face and neck exposed.

Sadani and her family greeted them and then Sadani explained the cups of tea. It is in three parts that represent the three parts of life. The first cup is bitter like life, the second sweet as love and the third is a cold tea, soft/cold like death. The group would have these three cups of tea daily and at every new meeting and location they visited. It was nice to have it explained in such detail. Then the recollections and stories would began, they were dark and some horrors of the dark side of hate in human nature. It was a long night, and the team was ready for sleep as soon as they arrived back at their hotel.

CHAPTER
SIX

To Find a Husband

The next day was the start of the days filled with meetings. Off to the Harbor Port and Water Distillery, a Social Eco-Development project. The Harbor Port was beautiful with lots of expansion under the new King. It was twice the size it was in 2005 and had a large fish market. They got to visit on a Sunday, of which Danell was very glad the market was empty. Even with just flat tables and superior cleanliness she could image all the fish and chopping that would occur. It was huge - they were shown the process it used- all computerized and high tech, a well-oiled machine. It was a big project that brought lots of jobs and increased income from the export of the fish.

After the port they drove to a lunch meeting at the home of De Wali-Mr. Mohomed Jelmous, governor. He was a wonderful man and passionate about his area and the projects they were working on. The group entered into a very large home, ornate yet uncluttered, a simplistically elegant style. They sat down to plates full of pistachios, almonds, sweet treats and a bottle of water. They all began to talk, and in came the tea (for a tea addict, Morocco is heaven). They were again served warm green tea with mint.

They discussed the **autonomy** plan between the Polisario and Morocco, the programs for the children, projects for entrepreneurs and also the ways that Danell's group could aid the country and cities. There were many items discussed and Danell was able to discuss the "Abandon Children" and what she could offer the orphanage (art lessons, supplies and a quilt for each child). De Wali was excited and said he would love the aid and asked if she could also bring a teacher that could teach the staff how to care for children. (To bathe, with homework, etc.) He told her they recently had a skin disease that spread quickly and they had to burn all the sheets and get new bedding. For a girl with a very over-active imagination she had to keep from making a face and stop her fingers from wanting to scratch a **physiologica**l itch had covered her arms.

De Wali's group shared their PowerPoint presentation of all the positive work initiatives that have occurred following the Kings Activities.

This local group has been able to make big **sustainable** change in a short period of time, it was impressive. After the presentation it was time to leave the sitting and meeting area and head into the dinner room as it was time for eating. They went into the eating room for pleasant conversations and food. Danell was excited by the many courses and the first was a large platter of a cold variety of salads: corn, carrot, cucumber. The platters were large and filled the center of the table. All ate from the one platter; you simply plunge your spoon into the bowl and eat. It was a true family style of sharing a meal. Danell remembered the bathroom rules and use of hands and not toilet paper. One must be culturally sensitive to use the right hand for eating and greeting and the left for "cleaning." So to all the natural lefties practice dominate use with the right hand to avoid any embarrassing moments when in certain countries.

Laughter was abundant as were the unusual stares. The De Wali continued to pass Danell more to eat every time her spoon was empty. It was explained that Moroccan women were preferred to be fat. Women would even illegally get cortisone shots to help them get fatter making them more attractive for the men. As he pointed to Danell, even before translation, she knew what he was saying. When translated in depth his words made her laugh and also become a little blush over her meager form. He was saying Danell was too thin and would never find Moroccan husband; he told her to gain weight, to be fat. He talked of the power of women- "they vote and there is the March of Women". Sahrawi women have a big role within the culture. Then came the next platter of food. A gorgeous array of seafood was very popular as this region was known for their fish. There was such variety laid out with fish kabobs, shrimp kabobs, fish fillet (a white fish, a nice mild fish). In the center of the platter was un-breaded calamari, Danell's first time to eat this un-breaded and it was very good. It was truly a breaking of bread type of meal as they talked about the people of this area and the culture. It was a meal filled with laughter and joy! As would be the case for many of the meetings, Danell noticed they were the only women, not just at the table but in the buildings they attended.

The final meal platter was a traditional couscous bowl; it was not a small cereal bowl but an expansive large platter, probably two feet in diameter. It was stacked full in a multi-layered food formation with the bottom housing the couscous, cooked carrots and zucchini. As the layers grew and you made your way up to the top it was layered with camel meat. Everyone was again given a large spoon, and you just ate, everyone off the same dish, a large double dipping family, and yet amazing. They just ate and ate, and talked and every time Danell's spoon was empty the De Wali would spoon more food on and in Arabic remind her that she must gain weight to get fat to be married. He was caring about her future by helping her food intake, Danell found it **endearing**. Each time it made her smile and laugh a little inside. And let there be more, another platter came, this bowl was filled of fruits, as with all the others filled means it was topped off to the rim and then made into a mound- no- more of a mountain. This final bowl was filled with bananas, persimmons, plums, oranges, and pears. It was a wonderful four course meal and filled with traditional foods from the area and the culture, exactly what one should eat when traveling.

When they got up for departure, they were greeted with a line of people to say their goodbyes and the De Wali had a gift for each as they left. Another Moroccan **tradition** is gifting your visitors and this occurred at every meeting / location. Even though it was a tradition, it felt quite special and each gift was unique to the person and a memory for Danell of the area and experiences she had there. De Wali-Mr. Mohamed Jelmous gave her a velvet box with jewelry, and he opened the box and put a bracelet on her "skinny" wrist. In providing our gift he reminded her again to keep eating!

They left his home and crossed the street into a plaza and walked less than a block to a guarded street with gates for a couple more meetings. One of which was with President of a company

Mouland Alouat. They were welcomed into a room with a large conference table and they were told of the needs of the area. "There are a lot of needs, support from the government is just not enough, help is accepted." The way he thought they could help was to bring networks to the table, visit senators and congressman on behalf of the Sahrawi issue, help get "ambassadors" for the Sahrawi people in front of an international platform to support the autonomy plan.

As they stood to leave the quick meeting with the President, they were presented gifts again. This time a hand carved bracelet, a black and silver creation, and as Danell's was put on her wrist it fell off (they were created a certain size, as they are carved and non-adjustable). The President and Danell almost bumped heads as both quickly bent down to grab it. She said, "It is good it will work." He said, "No, no, no," and handed it to the man next to him. He told her that he would get a smaller one and it would be delivered to her hotel at 6pm and it was!

Tea, Golden Dates, and Goat Heads

Next on the list to attend was the Abandoned Children Orphanage, one of the places on Danell's "must-visit" since the trip was planned. This orphanage was unique because they ran it like a non-profit and raised their own funds; they did not receive government aid.

When they arrived they were lined up in a single file row and treated to a large communal bowl of camel milk, and very sweet golden dates. The milk was cold and Danell pursed her lips for a very small taste and not a gulp. She was nervous for the cold liquid hitting her intestines that never had the pleasure of camel milk. The dates were delicious.

They began a walking tour, sliding quietly throughout very clean halls and walking on top of what felt and appeared like marble flooring. There were cut outs under the stairs filled with sculptures created with built-ins from around the country, highlighting specific areas the children have come from. There were traditional stories told and location specific folklore so that the children knew where they had come from and had roots of their provinces in Morocco.

The group gently removed their shoes and entered a big open room, to sit on floor cushions. They all shared three cups of tea and sweets, talked of the program and what they could offer the children and community. They learned a little about the lives of the women who care to others children at this orphanage. Many of the children come from the streets and sometimes they are left at the gates of the orphanage. This was the perfect place for *Threading Hope* and *Highwire*; there were infant cribs in need of blankets and bedding needs - quilts for the older children. The older children could take the quilts with them when they left the orphanage, and the infant blankets could stay and get continually reused providing comfort and warmth to many children.

When the group stood up to head upstairs to visit the rooms where the children live and sleep. But one of the group members only had one shoe. The pair no longer remained, so the "den mothers" went looking, and returned with big smiles on their faces and a shoe in hand. One of the children walked by, slipped on the shoe and was walking around with an extra-large shoe on her tiny little feet. The laughter roared.

The rooms were set up for families-the children shared a room with the "den mother" creating a family unit within an orphanage. It was very organized, clean and had a home-like feel. Nancy had tiny Beanie Babies to give the younger children and they all reached with excitement. Danell watched as the children pulled their toys into their chest for a big hug. While watching the large group's joy she suddenly felt as if she had eyes on her. Seconds later she felt arms around her, a little girl latched on. Danell bent down and the little girl put her hands around Danell's neck and her ear to her chest. "I *am not sure why I did, but I started humming and she held on tightly and gently at the same time. She listened to my heart beat, my humming and swayed, we swayed together. In this moment without words, without toys in hand or goods to give, this very human moment of connection and love with someone you have never met...my heart cried with a joy unique to this experience*." It was a very special, very moving moment. When it was time to move on, the others toured different rooms; Danell just sat in that room alone with that young girl and held her. Her den mother was in the doorway, and she smiled at her with warmth. In that moment although only three people were in that room, it was filled with so much light, so much love. It would have been easy to cry but Danell did not as this child had enough tears. Right now this child just wanted humming and hugs...she could do that!

The others came back and it was time to go, it literally took two den mothers to pull the child off of Danell, which was heart breaking. Danell had let go but the child would not and she had to be pulled from her arms, ouch. There was such strength and wisdom in this little child at just three or four years old. She looked deeply into Danell's eyes and tears fell from hers. She did not scream she was not having a tantrum; just a quiet solitary tear fell with power and statement. Danell would long hold this moment and her memory. As she left the room Danell let her own quiet tear fall and lived quietly in that moment all the way back to the hotel. Sometimes you need only to be in your own mind, and some moments need to be held close until you are ready to share them.

The afternoon was spent meeting a woman who was changing women's lives and creating a network of women entrepreneurs in Morocco. Hajbouha Zoubeir runs a foundation for the women of Laâyoune as president of the Association of Business Women in Laâyoune (AMFED). The foundation "...supports creation of enterprises directed by women and young people and assisting women in rural areas to become literate and financially independent."

She was also a member of the Union of Feminine Action (UAF) and actively participated in fighting for human rights of Sahrawi women. The reach and passion she had was radiating and inspirational.

For dinner the group headed to Zoubeir's Restaurant in a tent, a new business venture of Hajbouha and her husband, a lovely experience. They traveled about 15 kilometers out of the city and into the desert for a traditional nomadic meal within a large canvas tent. Not as one would imagine when you hear tent, it was more of open air elegance. They removed their shoes, sat on cushions placed on elaborate rugs and dined on silver platters.

They were served traditional rounds of tea from painted glass cups and silver tea pots heated over hot stones piled on the desert sands. Out there in the middle of the desert they sat as traditional nomads, just short of delivery by camel; it felt very unique and a little like living in a chapter from *The Alchemist* by Paulo Coelho.

The hosts knew of Danell not eating meat, being a vegetarian, and when the large platter was served piled with couscous topped with a full bodied cooked goat, she was delivered her own tiny platter. Piled couscous and topped with a chicken... she bent her head and thanked them for the lovely cooked meal. Lucky she had a great seat-mate that let her quietly peel the chicken and put a little on her plate to play with and a large chunk onto the other plate so that it would get eaten. Chickens, you see, are "not meat as they are chickens," white meat so not meat at all. (This was how the meat was explained) All the roasted vegetables and grains were enough to fill anyone. It was a unique meal and a wondrous experience. This was how a meal should be eaten, with laughter and spoons from a large communal table, draped with rugs, silks and hours of conversation.

It was time to fly out of Laâyoune and back to Casablanca for the drive to Rabat. In Rabat they would spend their evening in La Tour Hassan hotel but not to rest just yet as they were off to another dinner meeting.

CHAPTER
EIGHT

Women Leaders & the Kings Council

They met in the private home of then parliament
member Zahra Chagaf, a woman in a leadership
position in parliament. Danell and her group of 4
were not the only guests honored to speak with
Zahra, and when they arrived they were
introduced to a large group of women from
Washington State – Center for Women &
Democracy (CWD).

As they sat with in discussions, the brightness
from the women of the CWD was almost
blinding. There was such dedication in this
group to build women's leadership, and advance
participation and representation in local and
global affairs. From just the group of women
Danell met here, mothers and daughters to
grandmothers - the global promotion of women
in leadership coming out of Washington State
was powerful in fostering global citizens.

At the time of this writing the world experienced a great loss. Zahra Chagaf moved on from this worldly life, a deep loss for many. Zahra rest in peace and know that your fight brought women in leadership to the forefront and good will continue in your name - honor all the good you did and gave.

The conversations were wonderful as were the connections. One of the women said there was a lot Danell could share of her art, writing, travel and would be a perfect fit for an upcoming evening event. A call was made and she was approved for the invite to leave early with a small group of CWD women to attend a private discussion in the home of Fatema Mernissi. Fatema is an author, woman's rights activist, art therapist... world renowned feminist. One famous and widely translated work by Fatema is: *Why Islam Scares the West.* Needless to say Danell felt honored to be with the handful of women selected to meet with her.

Born in the 1940's Fatema Mernissi grew up in a harem and learned oppressiveness first hand. Her dedication to women's rights began very early and continued to bloom through learning of women's freedoms in other countries and the lack of it in her home country, Morocco.

She writes in English and French, and with many of her works translated into various languages she has made a strong impact in the Muslim and

Western worlds. There were philosophical discussions while surrounded by color and beautiful arts, sweets and tea in her private home. As an activist and a writer she provided evidence and extensive research deep into issues she wrote about. Just to hear her talk it was easy to become **mesmerized**. Not only was the content in her arguments enthralling, her genuine passion shined out through a very dynamic smile. Her life was *art* from her creative art works to her writing - all represented an overall passion for living.

She spoke of the power of women and discussed that cooking was a woman's power; she gave advice to all the women, "you can start your own story." She then talked on travel and experiencing culture and said, "When you go to foreign countries, the further away you are, the more you discover who you really are. See yourself – truth in the mirror of the stranger!" It was a powerful statement and one that would radiate in Danell's truth of travel for the rest of her life. She loved the rawness of self that was reflected by strangers in travel.

*   *   *

Mohammed V Foundation

During Danell's time spent in Morocco, she learned of the work being done with women, children, education, and access for the poor to life's necessities. In the "Western Sahara" they visited many programs that were helped by and started by Mohammed V Foundation. Danell learned about how *Highwire* and *Threading Hope* could support in many ways. Although she did not meet with the King himself, maybe one day, but she did meet with the King's council for inspiring talks of future collaborations in humanitarian work.

"The foundation's main objective is to fight against all forms of poverty and social marginalization and to endeavor to provide relief to the destitute and to those living in precarious conditions, using all possible means, and undertaking, in particular, solidarity-based actions."

At the table discussions, this meeting felt like home, as they discussed objectives back and forth with a collective mindset of bettering people's lives. Danell had found her voice and audience at this meeting and really got a platform to discuss her ideas. When she spoke of *Highwire* and *Threading Hope* and what it could

offer, the council was excited and genuinely
interested in the programs. During the week
they had been to a few other locations and she
felt that it was not her platform; she often sat
back, but this was exactly what her foundations
were for. It was a wonderful meeting and a few
of the women said, "You have a great program."
Danell felt good to be at the table when
excitement was high and ideas were flowing.

The council explained the process. When ready
to partner, one writes to the foundation and
describes the objective, what equipment that
would be needed and if the objective is liked by
the foundation, they will say yes. The proposal
would include the aid and what could be done
together. They only accept new items for
donations, and when Danell talked in detail
about the handmade quilts and how they were
not purchased but made with dedication and
love, and have not been used by another, they
were very excited for future ventures... as was
Danell! They thought that the art supplies and
quilts would be a perfect fit for the orphanages
and hospitals, in her heart the perfect locations.
There were over 200 orphanages supported by
this council, *Threading Hope* could spend a
lifetime in providing quilts to them all. So Danell
decided that her focus when she returned would
be for the most rural, hard to access, and most in
need orphanages and hospitals.

The foundation was unique and showed the commitment of the Moroccan people - in that the King himself presided over the foundation as effective president. To further his dedication he supported Solidarity Microfinance programs that provided micro credits in the field, giving the opportunity for skills / training and sharing such training with their neighbors. The benefits and main goal of the training: "Aims to promote and support income-generating activities and changing socio-economic conditions of micro entrepreneurs." The most impressive fact about it all was the forethought into the future, creating programs that have longevity, and sustainability built in.

Danell's group arrived in country years after His Majesty the King, Mohammed VI's State of the Nation Address, when he spoke of his dedication to the poor and struggling. During this visit Danell was able to visit many of these "fields of action" projects and see the ability that one man had to help create and continue. It was easy to find yourself inspired by the motivation, and the commitment of the people and the King. They have made so much happen.

*　　　*　　　*

Danell knew she would find herself in Morocco again for a more extended time. There was so much of the country she had yet to see, although the trip was amazing she also learned so much. Danell wanted to see more of the country, she did not make it to the mountains of Fez or the northern villages, and this was how she knew she would be back. So much to see and do, so many people in rural areas she did not get to, and now that she had a good direction of how *Threading Hope* and *Highwire* can be of use...let the planning begin!

HAITI

Dominican Republic

o Port-au-Prince

Pétionville

REPUBLIQUE D'HAITI
ENTREE
0401
3 0 JUIN 2010
27
Aeroport Port-au-Prince
IMMIGRATION / EMIGRATION

Capital:
Port-au-Prince

Language:
French &
Creole

CHAPTER
NINE

Sunsets & Smog to Clinics & Compounds

Landing in PAP
Port-au-Prince Airport

Within minutes puddles appeared flowing from her underarms as a quick reminder of the difference in her then Arizona home of dry heat and Haiti's humidifying bubble. She exited the plane on the tarmac and walked into the terminal to claim her bag. There was a large group of people, all waiting to grab baggage.

Danell's little black suitcase made its way slowly on the U-shaped belt, she grabbed it and attempted to extend the handle, finding only half the metal was present, the other half- completely gone. One of the airport staff looked over at her, and they both raised their shoulders and laughed. Exiting the terminal was just as interesting. They were all surrounded by UN guards and chain link fencing that was keeping

the public 100 yards from the terminal exit.
Danell thought maybe that was how it always
was but she found out later that the airport was
fenced and the guards were all encompassing
because the day before a UN peacekeeper was
shot at the airport. Looking back into her
memory Danell cannot recall if he was killed or
injured, but the presence of armed guards made
for an intense arrival.

*　　　　　*　　　　　*

The creaks of her cot mimicked the sounds of her
bones as she stretched out from long flights, for a
quick nap in her tent. Sporadic tics came from
the overheating fan that attempted to cool the
mad rush of sweat engulfing her body as it was
re-learning the meaning of humidity! Home was
a tent on a concrete driveway of a gated house in
Port au Prince. The bedrooms within the actual
house were rented out to doctors and nurses; it
helped to fund the projects of MMRC (Materials
Management Relief Corps) – the grassroots NGO
Danell was working with.

A little flash back to how she ended up here in a
tent, behind a gate in Haiti. A friend of hers from
the high-fashion world, Paul Sebring (fashion
photographer) was co-founder of MMRC and
moved to Haiti after the earthquake of 2010.

They worked together in Phoenix on past projects of her couture company, dl-couture, and did charity shots with a gown she created from AZ Cardinals game jerseys that was signed by the entire NFC team. (The gown was later auctioned and the funds were delivered to the hospital Partners in Malawi). It was during this shoot that they realized they had a lot in common with the direction of their lives. Her fashion company was built on humanitarian work and only created 13 custom gowns a year giving her the time for other passions, *Threading Hope* and *Highwire*.

Paul found his passion in people and capturing it more on a level of newsworthy photography than high fashion. It was over Thai food in Phoenix that they planned to work together again in Haiti. (Many months after Haiti, he was in South America doing more humanitarian work. Fast track about a year after that and he was continuing his drive to help others by going back to school to complete his nursing credentials to help yet more people!) Travel and philanthropy can change a person, they can find the truest tune that plays from their heart, the connecting rhythm that flows within us all, directions can change as can purpose, and it is quite a beautiful thing.

She lay in bed, having showered for the night as sweat beads followed the deep creases of her neck and flowed to a puddle at the base of her throat. Here was a muggy heat filled with car pollution that made breathing and self-cooling very difficult. She felt as if her body was liquefying and the cot would sift out the solids as she slowly dripped through.

*   *   *

Today was bank day, which was perfect timing as Danell needed to exchange her American cash to local currency Gourde (HGT). Travel in Haiti for her was usually in the back of truck bed, coated in sunscreen wearing UV sunglasses, and drinking lots of water...it was a blessing to find shade and fans moving the stagnant swampy air.

Even during a day of necessary errands one can see the devastation caused by the earthquake and learn of stories where collapsed buildings were ravaged for the guns and supplies inside, but the bodies remained undug. There were certain parts of the city that one could still smell what was buried beneath layers of weighted concrete block when the heat began to reach it...there was just too much devastation. Locals were trying to clean it up, many roads were being cleared and on any day there was someone working, trying, but the amount of damage and support for reconstruction did not equate.

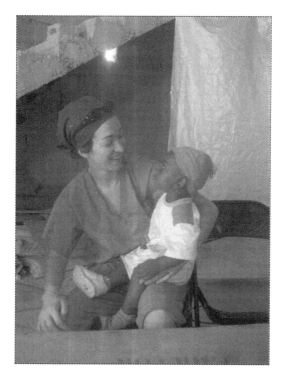

There was still daylight and she was invited to work with Kelly and Erica, two nurses giving vaccinations to the children at a local school and orphanage run by Junior B. Danell swapped out her sweat-riddled clothing and threw on some of the scrubs (left by other volunteers) and they were off. As they began preparation for departure she looked down at her borrowed scrubs and was greeted by leftover blood drops. She looked up, and Paul said, "It's clean, no worries, and it is Haiti." He ended with a caring but real smile from a man that has already spent months here. So when in Haiti, Danell wore that top with love and for a couple days as needed!

She got the best job once they arrived, well she helped hand out what was needed, but then she got to hold the children and just watch the grins grow across to full-on smiles. One little boy stared at her face so intently and then slowly moved his hands over her cheek bones, nose, and around her jaw. It was one of those very moving, very human moments that children are so great at providing. He was studying her pale skin and facial structure.

They made a make shift clinic in a simple concrete room. (Later they were shown the mixture included whatever could be found, be it cement, cardboard, chip bags, literally anything that could be combined in the mixture). The room had half-completed stairs where they were joined by a couple chickens that ran away as the patients filtered in. Patients entered the waiting room from behind a sheet that provided a simple element of privacy. Occasionally they would go to get medicine from a crate and have to swat away a chicken or two before dispensing could continue. Once the locals heard about the impromptu clinic, they got many visitors that were willing to wait for hours to be seen.

As the day was wrapping up, Junior B played some music and then a few of the school girls came in and there in the middle of what was just the clinic, they began to do a beautifully choreographed waltz full of spins laughter and joy! The work of Junior B. and his sister Rose was helping so many young girls find education! They were doing great things here and are dedicated to a life of aid and the compassion was just a genuine part of who they are.   (Later it would be Junior B. who caught Danell as she passed out - stay tuned)

Back at the "compound," (the house and all houses have 10-foot walls and gates and barbwire that surround them) Danell ventured up uneven metal slats that created a make- shift ladder to the roof. She took snacks, water, and electrolyte powder to enjoy the sunset over the ocean in the distance. She did not know at the time how special this moment would be, but it would be the only time the sky was clear enough from smog to see the sunset, to see the sky, to see the sun, for the rest of her time in Haiti.

Day one ended with "campfire" talks from the team. Big-Paul (Danell's friend from AZ), Little-Paul the other MMRC co-founder, Alan-Staats, a photographer down here doing great coverage of the devastation and the hopes of the country, a few of the nurses, Kelly and Erica, and the locals that were on the team, Little Junior, Ralph and Eli! They set up a plan for when Danell was to head off to Medishare Pediatrics unit in the morning and teach a therapeutic art lesson to the children there for *Highwire*, and provide quilts to families being healed post-earthquake for *Threading Hope*. They discussed the deliveries to be made of OTC (over the counter) medications for MMRC check-ups at orphanages. This little grassroots foundation made a large difference and Danell would be involved in many functions during her short time here. From hospital transfers, to art lessons, to quilt deliveries, to tent city clinic hygiene deliveries- that turn into snapping on her gloves and helping to stop a bleeding artery, you never knew what each day held.

When the days slowed she questioned what she was doing, as down time was not normal, she should be out doing something, she was used to one thing after another. When Danell got a chance to breathe, she wanted a project....be careful what you ask for...all in all Haiti was amazing and opened her mind, even gave her a new take on how to repair a broken truck with a metal rod and a rock.

CHAPTER
TEN

HOA: Hospitals, Orphanages, and Art

A big thank you to whoever invented the suitcase with wheels...thank you! Danell arrived at Medishare for a four and half-hour block of time to work with the children in the pediatrics unit. She had loaded her roll-able suitcase filled with art kits (backpacks stuffed with coloring books, crayons, pencils, erasers and more). She parked it in the corner, squeezed lovingly between a baby crib and the wall, finding space in an already maxed-out unit was a feat in itself. She was left to work one-on-one with each child. It was chaotic and with nurses flowing in and out, the care of timed feedings to the premature infants and the shuffle of care given to a child with **hydroencephalitis**, all appeared as a well-planned dance. A waltz her wheeled suitcase glided throughout. The young child's hydrocephalic head continued to swell; the parents dropped her here and never returned.

The staff and local mothers took turns holding her to give her some comfort until her passing. Danell spent an hour one day, until her arms fell asleep, embracing the child and cleaning the seeping that escaped from her eyes due to pressure, there was nowhere for all the liquid to go. It was heart breaking as her life would look so different if a shunt surgery were available here.

The first young man Danell worked with, for *Highwire*, was covered in scars and had painfully misshapen legs from crushed knees. His home had collapsed on him in the earthquake. He lost his entire family in the destruction, his scars had healed, but movement was limited and function was aided from pain medication. During her entire 4 hours there she did not hear his cries of pain. He hid them until she left and then the debilitating screams would echo. Danell was outside awaiting her ride, he thought he had left. In the many days she returned, she always made a stop at Andre's bedside. One day they enjoyed a parking lot stroll as she pushed him in circles in his wheelchair. They imagined the courtyard was a large park; in reality it was gray, small and was filled with rushed hospital personnel and parking, but they still saw the beauty and enjoyed great laughs every time a wheelie occurred.

The permanent scars on his face would never hide the pain he went through. During the earthquake crushing of his scalp occurred. It pulled skin and a scar floated across his entire forehead. There was such strength in this young man and his scars were not disfiguring in Danell's eyes and added such power to the calmness in his smile, one that reminded her why she does what she is doing. When crayons and a coloring book can bring this much joy to one life...Andre may have been thankful and inspired from the quilt made by my grandmother, or the backpack full of art supplies...but Danell could only hope he knew that he was her inspiration. He is why *Threading Hope* and *Highwire* are here!

It was in Haiti that Danell learned how important the labels are on the backs of the quilts. This was the first major trip for both *Highwire* and the first delivery trip for *Threading Hope*. The co-founder of *Threading Hope* Danell's mother, Kristina Green and Danell decided that the quilts should have labels. There would be a space for them to write the name of the quilter who donated and the name of the person that was receiving it. At the time of the decision they did not know the impact these labels would have. A young couple in the pediatrics unit had a child with a physical disability, her legs were severely bowed and her grunts combined with crossed eyes led one to assume there was a mental capacity disability as well. The mother laid the quilt on her lap, set her child gently on top and then looked up with a proud smile beaming from ear to ear. Later in the week when her daughter was allowed to go home, the mother started packing up all their belongings and the local hospital staff told her, "The quilt stays here; it is not yours." She showed them the back of the quilt with her daughter's name on it to prove that they were not stealing, that it was given to her family. They were allowed to take it home and our *Threading Hope* quilts will forever have labels and family names written in permanent marker.

A day of work in Haiti was never one thing, your days were packed and you were needed in many ways. One time when Danell was picked up at the hospital in the jalopy of a truck, they headed off to help deliver supplies, and the truck broke down. They shuffled out and tried to find shade to sit in. Little Paul and Big Paul opened the hood and Lil' P grabbed a rock (a piece of rubble in the street) and a metal pipe, aimed both at the starter box, and bam, bam... voilà it started! Mechanics, man they make a killing stateside, if all that was needed was a rock and rod.... they were laughing about it for a while! She would never know if he thought it would really work, was a talented aim or if it was a little luck, like pounding on the TV and then all of sudden you have a picture. But none the less she loved it, breakdown and repair, Haitian style.

Later that evening, still the same day, they visited an orphanage that Lil' Paul had done a lot of work with. He had helped build beds, bunkhouses and visited them often providing for needs they might have.   The group arrived and the children surrounded him; they were full of nothing but love.   Up the stairs on the landing into the main house the children built kites on the porch in the night air, using the glow of the inside house lights. They were making them out of plastic bags (like the grocery bags back home) - quite resourceful. They played games and hung out for a few hours and then went to shower and bed.

The next day they headed north to the mountains. They had boxes of donated clothing, blankets and medical supplies for an orphanage in Fermathe. The roads were rough, dirt and rocks flew around them as they drove. They pushed forward and heard the thudding of a flat tire. As they came upon a little city / town with a few buildings, even in this tiny roadside town there were people waiting for flats with replacements to repair your tire. They piled out of the truck, not to venture too far away, as the back was loaded with boxes of supplies, but they needed shade.

Danell leaned back into a metal door, its heat radiated into her and the odor of hot urine engulfed her sense of smell. Looking around at the green trees and lush landscape you are fooled into thinking you will be surrounded by fresh air. The tire was fixed and they went on.

They later transferred the supplies into another truck that could travel the "bad roads" into the hills where the children were located. She laughed as she was made aware that they were on the "good" roads. The orphanage truck went left; they went right to meet with Fritz a local sculptor.

He did well for himself by any societal standards and lived life on his own terms. He had a nice house on the edge of the mountain, his friends would come by and they all sat around talking politics. Fritz spent thousands of his own money every year buying trees and planting them throughout the hills to bring back the lush beauty of his homeland and cleaner air. He was very passionate about his movement and it was utterly refreshing as his hope filtered into his fellow man on how to save Haiti through the trees! Making the world a little more beautiful with passion and hope, not to mention his very well sculpted statues of women that look as if they were gliding on air, it was a pleasure to meet Fritz - a modern day Johnny Appleseed.

On the way back down the mountain, they hiked along a tiny path, and ducked under jutting bridges of connected houses to find their way to the farthest hut in the back corner to the home of Mary Louis. She was a woman that had no health care, doctors were too far away, and the large cancerous tumor continued to grow, protruding from her stomach. She lived in a hut made from pallets and corrugated metal slats. Her front door was a sheet to cover the opening. She rested on a coverless bed and could barely walk but made her way outside to thank them greatly for the quilt provided to her from a *Threading Hope* donation. Her daughter (probably in her 30's) gave deep squeeze hugs and thanked them. She placed the quilt gently on her mother's bed and her mother lay down to rest on the new layer of comfort and care.

The following day they had an organizing day of deliveries. They were to organize and unpack the new OTC medications and get the pallets ready for pick up from some of the smaller foundations MMRC works with based in the more rural areas. These other foundations help get supplies out into the field where needed without all the red tape. They get so much done here, it fascinated Danell. Once the other organizations had stopped by to pick up their pallets full of supplies, the MMRC group was off for a day of relaxing at the Oloffson Hotel, to celebrate the 4th of July.

The hotel was stunning and the old architecture looked similar to that of New Orleans. They had our cold drinks, and spent the day at the swimming pool. Danell even tried a local fried root that everyone raved about. It was good, although the oil had the flavor of fish and tasted weeks past due for a change. This was when she first met Mike, a young man that had just returned to work in Haiti after a vacation to Argentina. They all knew what brought him back, his love interest; she was still here working.

The next morning they were called to help transfer a patient with kidney failure to the hospital for dialysis. Although foundations all around the world had sent tons of money for expensive ambulances, they did not get used, and if they did use them the ambulances were not outfitted for emergencies. They were told, "They are working on this problem." MMRC did transports in the bed of their tiny junk of a truck. It saved lives and got people from point A to B.

After the day of rest and enjoyment at the pool Danell was ready for work, but other than the transport, there was nothing on the calendar. Lil' Paul had a good handle on the schedule and kept them very busy. He had left the night before to complete a project in France. He was a master carpenter and gets privately hired this was where his funding came from for his work of the heart. The team had a meeting before he left, but once he was gone they laid around. Danell took issue with the non-movement, and tried not to ruminate, but that did not work. She used the satellite phone and considered changing her flight to return home, as she did not come all the way here to sit behind a gated wall and stare at the ceiling of her tent. It was now late afternoon and she was not doing well with her own psyche, when Mike popped back around on a little 125cc motorbike. She vented her frustration as they shared a cup of Matte tea from his Argentinian trip. He said to Danell, "You are not going home, instead let's make deliveries." They grabbed their backpacks, loaded them down with hygiene kits, hopped on the kick-start bike and headed to tent city hospitals to deliver needed supplies.

It was a little surreal, as motorbike travel tends to be, you are so much closer to the lives you are experiencing. The roads were littered with potholes, they had to dodge and weave and dodge again. The extent of the piled up trash and smells of rotting food that filled the streets you would think could ruin the ride, but somehow the weaving in and out on the motorbike with a breeze, and local music pumping to the beat of your heart, it was wonderful. It felt like a soundtrack to life in Haiti and through the dust and grit that surrounded them, Danell could not stop smiling. It was a peaceful, beautiful moment in time. This was what she needed. Her days in Haiti were numbered and she wanted to be of use, the entire time!

As they arrived, the hillside was a vast sea of tents, for as far as one could see tents were stacked one upon the other. The sight was humbling. They arrived at Petionville and stopped at the tent clinic to deliver the kits and came upon a man that had "fallen" on a glass bottle. He had a chunk out of his back that was gushing blood. He came right up to Mike and Danell to ask for help in English. They sat him on a cot and applied pressure. Mike tried to get the local nurses or staff to pay attention and help him, but they just ignored his pleas as the injured man spoke fluent English and was Rastafarian, two things that they were told was looked down upon. They all carried their "kits," plastic gloves, mask, and first aid supplies. It was just part of being there at that time; you never left home without it. And it saved this man's life. They sat for a while and talked, he spoke with a litany of stories, and Mike told Danell later that it was a common story of "falling" but it was most likely violence that occurred in "tent city". Mike then asked her how much of the city she had seen, and if she had seen the demolished capitol. She had not, so they headed to view it.

It was right across from one of the more dangerous crime-riddled tent cities so they did not get off the bike and paused only long enough for Danell to snap photos. They then headed to enjoy the needed medicine of Haiti...ice cold drinks to cool the body in the heat. They discussed each other's travels, work within other countries and what they do to make a living. Mike was just 22 (at the time) worked on yachts for part of the year and then traveled the world for the other part doing humanitarian work all over. She was utterly impressed with him and all that he has done in such a short span of his life.

They headed back to the MMRC home and were shocked to find the man from earlier in the day, the man they had helped stop bleeding, was now sprawled across the picnic table, profusely bleeding from his back again. This time it was a big bleeder, they all took turns applying pressure but it looked to be an artery nick as it literally shot blood up into the air. After they got the bleeding to stop that afternoon, he did not rest and it got worse. They loaded him into their emergency vehicle (lil truck) and rushed to the hospital as the bleeding would not stop this time. He needed medical help, they dropped him at Medishare and the doc asked Danell for the run down. Later he asked where she studied...um...it was bleeding...pressure was needed...the school of common sense...they both laughed. She has no medical training but has been faced with some medical decisions to help in developing countries and during accidents at home that have prompted the question from medics about her training.

 Little did Danell know she would be back in a few days to see this same doctor, except she would be a patient! It began to rain on the drive home. It was nice to relax to the rumble of the rain as it hit their tin roof, and then the sound of the thunder mixed with the downpour. She thought she would sleep well tonight!

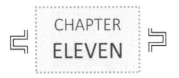

CHAPTER
ELEVEN

On Call...

ON CALL... when partnering with a group that has already made a country wide reputation as "the go to team"; one never knows what might come your way! Danell awakened, put on her scrubs and side pouch kit. This kit was a great little cloth bag, which attached around the waist, that Danell's grandmother made for her to hold plastic gloves, gauze, face masks and other needed supplies. They left to pick up an ambulance to transport a TB patient from the hospital to the TB tent. As they arrived for drop off, a man was rolled by with a sheet covering his face. He was dead and a very thin - life slowed as his body passed on the gurney. It looked as if he came from the direction of the large canvas tent that they were headed towards. Danell readjusted her mask, headed to the back of the ambulance and began the transfer.

Masks are a must when transporting patients with Tuberculosis. They entered a tent set up on the grounds of the hospital, a large area with cots, and every bed full. The woman running the ward has dedicated so much of herself to saving the lives of TB patients in Haiti. It was a heartbreaking and heartwarming place at the same time. They made the transfer and headed home to organize more supplies.

Meals could be about as adventuresome as the days in Haiti; dinner tonight consisted of a vegetarian MRE. Danell grew up in a military family but they did not fantasize about the amazing meals that MREs supply. It was actually not too bad, and kind of fun, and at least she knew not to chew the gum. (As some others found out, it has a bit of a laxative quality).

One cannot always tell when a storm rolls in, because the gray storm hue was the daily smog, but the sounds gave awareness to what was coming. The skies began to rumble again tonight. Eli grabbed his soccer ball, he and Danell exchanged a look and it was on, soccer in the drive way in the rain. This was one of her magical memories from Haiti. Eli was a young Haitian teenager that lived with the group and worked with MMRC. Lil' P brought him home from the gas station one day to work –learning he had no family - he became a part of theirs. His English was not strong and her Haitian non-existent, but no words were needed with the ball in hand – she completely understood. Everyone thought they were crazy as they were soaked, and yet played on for at least 30 minutes. Eventually the drops lessened and they thought maybe it was a short sprinkle, but that was short lived and the downpour continued creating delight.   Then lightning caught up with the thunder and sounded really close, they thought that maybe they should not stand in the rain any longer!

Day 7, hard to believe it has only been a week; the amount of life that had been experienced in such a short time was a reminder of why she does this work, why Danell needed it!

Last night they hosted some late night visitors from IFA (Israeli Flying Aid) that have been working with Glorious Cross Orphanage. The going ons and accusations of what was occurring there was completely mind blowing. They had been asked to visit the orphanage the next day and take the children who were being refused medicine and lacking proper care out to the hospitals. IFA had a volunteer at the orphanage for about six months and there was worry that some of the children were so sickly they may be close to death. The problem was not that they didn't have a chance to go to the hospital; it was reported that the orphanage took them, got the proper medication, but upon return refused to give the children their medicine, instead choosing to sell it. You can either choose to accept what you hear as truth or at least something that needs reviewed, anytime you are dealing with accusations you do not witness it is always a sensitive situation, and does not mean it occurred and does not mean it did not. The physical condition of the girls- they were made to walk around in just their underwear, not provided clothing unless they were aware visitors were coming; it was only then the nuns scramble to save face, and bathe them quickly. This occurred when MMRC arrived and they took their time letting them in, as they tried to prepare the façade.

The drinking water was a hole in the ground; the concern was its being uncovered and the bacteria and dead stuff inside could not be healthy to give to the children. Physically the most heart breaking part of this orphanage was that it did not shock, it looked like much of Haiti, and the destruction the city underwent and was still facing.

They arrived at the orphanage and began to walk the grounds. The caretakers brought the children out to line them up, but one of the ladies from IFA went into rooms and located a little girl that had a severely high fever. MMRC ended up finding seven children that needed to go to the doctors, fevers mostly and one with fungus that covered her body and face.

After the investigation, they were lining up the children to take with them, and Danell was holding a young girl whose belly protruded. The child was so hot with a fever but something felt wrong, not with her, but with Danell. She walked over to my friend Big Paul and said, "I feel dizzy, take her," he reached out and grabbed the child, and the last thing she remembered saying was, "I can't see!" When she came back to consciousness, she was lying on the ground being held up by Junior B. She was told he caught her as she collapsed. Many eyes were on her as she slowly came back into reality. From those around some say she was out, not breathing for 10 seconds, others say it was 30 seconds. All she knew was she unconscious, she had never blacked out and collapsed before and was just so thankful that she felt funny first and was able to hand over the little girl before she fell.

Because of what MMRC does here they had IV's and some gear in the truck. Big Paul sat Danell down tied an IV to the roof, and began fluids to help jump start her body. Another guy ran to the street to buy cookies and a soda to bounce up her sugars. She had been drinking lots of water, eating her electrolyte blocks and using water electrolyte additives ever since she arrived. But her shirt was soaked and her spine had a waterfall of fluids filtering down right before she passed out, but she knew none of these signs, had no background knowledge to prepare for her body's reaction.

She sat and shared her cookies with the orphaned girls as the team continued the work and started to load the children into the trucks to take them to the hospital. Once they got all the kids into the care of the doctors, Big Paul came back to the truck and helped take Danell out. He carried the IV. Dr. Kendrick Lopez (the man from the other night who helped with the bleeder) took her to their volunteer room set up with cots where the doctors and nurses slept. He put Danell onto a cot, covered her, checked her over, hooked her up to another IV and said it appeared to be vaso-vagal, heat exhaustion, nerves, and dehydration. She went through three IV bags or was it five; she cannot recall. She was sent home with ORS packets to add to water that tasted like salt and for a girl who does not even stock her kitchen cabinets with salt, it tasted gross but was needed, so she made a face with every gulp.

Looking back she remembered that day she was drinking a lot but her entire body was lined with sweat as a continuous drip flowed over her creating a sheen coating on her skin. With the high heat and high humidity, her body could not adjust. She will forever react a little differently to heat, even dry heat; her tolerance to high outdoor temperatures would never be the same. She now could feel when her body was too hot and it has created a mild fear, one that will follow her when she is in a similar climate in Cuba years later. Part of her trip was plagued with the fear that she might pass out; it has not occurred again thankfully. She was told that a change in temperature regulation was normal; once you experienced heat exhaustion your internal temperate never quite cools the same.

Back at the compound, she ate a little dinner, and then headed off to bed early to get some rest! She was just a day away from flying home when she passed out, one day left. She still had art kits and a few quilts. The plan was to visit the new children in the pediatric ward at Medishare but none of them knew how she would be the next morning, would she have any energy?

When morning came she felt much better - not 100% but not 10% any longer either - so they packed the bags and headed back to the hospital. This was the same hospital they had come to the night before. Dr. K was on shift again; did this man ever sleep? He dealt with a lot every day, but still had a wonderful sense of humor! He asked a few questions, did a once over and said she was good, so off to the pediatric unit for some art and laughter!

It was bitter sweet, nice to be there again but with a realization that she would miss visiting these children and their desire to pull through and continue. This was one trait that all Haitians she met had in common. They were a hardy, strong people, and they had some of the best smiles and laughter!

At the time of this trip she was teaching at private school in Arizona for children with high functioning autism. The students in her classroom found out about her trip and wanted to raise funds for Haiti and help where it was most needed. She later received baggies of change, full of week's allowances. The students raised $160.00 for her to take to Haiti that they used to purchase 600 diapers for the infants, a great need. They then gave the diapers to the families of newborns that could not afford them. They were so grateful! These teenagers saved all they could and donated to families they had never met. It was a dream for Danell to see a new generation embracing philanthropy.

With only half a day of work at the hospital, she was still weak from the day before and needed a nap. They headed home to rest and pack for her quick approaching departure. That night they all went to dinner! It was a great way to end this trip. That evening she sat on the deck pondering over the week's events. She was surrounded by a down pour again; it drummed softly on the metal roof as Haiti's skies cried her tears.

The smog had lessened, and the burning of trash no longer filled her nasal cavity, but the rains would soon bring floods and wash away the lives of more. That year's hurricane season would be devastating as so many were still tent living on flood plains. (Six months later the news would discuss the effect of the flooding and the outbreaks of cholera). The size of the drops lessened, and then the rain quit, the silence was short before the bustle began again, the skies rumbled. As her stomach tried to heal from who knows what, a bug, the heat exhaustion, all the salts, the thunder laughed at her weakness, vibrated through her body and slowly called her to sleep. This was a little more relaxing than the soft rains of the desert to lull you into slumber, except it was lacking in smell, the magnificent smell of desert rain in Arizona. It was not a pure smell here, and at times the air was so thick and polluted that breathing could be congested.

She had met some truly fascinating people full of wisdom, passion and desire for humanity. This had been the flame needed to spark the dedication that would follow her and inspire her. As the kick off trip of *Threading Hope* and the first full kits kick-off for *Highwire*...it was beginning and it sure was beautiful.

She enjoyed her quiet humbling moments during the evenings as she put pen to paper and created navigation to the travels and experiences she had. Life really was meant to be lived and the energy of the Haitian people, and their smiles, oh the smiles would warm your heart. Danell's head was reaching towards the pillow for her last night in country. "Good night Haiti, thank you for your time, and sharing your light."

She flew home the next morning and would continue to release soot from her nose for five days after returning. Her lungs actually began to breathe with ease again two weeks after that.

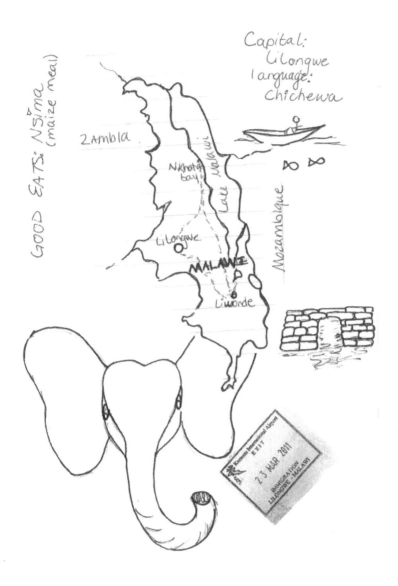

CHAPTER
TWELVE

AIDS destruction, Education's rebirth

The way that life lines itself up, is nothing short of mesmerizing and the older she gets the more Danell feels like she is on a continuous loop of It's a Small World ride at Disneyland. While shooting a FOX 10 Sports News segment with anchor Gayle Jansen on her Arizona Cardinals game jersey gown, dl-couture created for charity, Danell learned of Gayle's brother's work in Malawi, Africa. It was destined and a few years after the airing of the news coverage Danell and her mother found themselves in Malawi at Partners in Hope presenting a check from the auction of the gown, to Perry Jansen for the projects at the hospital and donating quilts to the Thandizo in-patient ward. They were also able to do art therapy classes for children with physical and mental disabilities at Children of Blessings Trust.

Danell and her mother were housed in the home of Brenda and Perry Jansen and shared their dinner table with their children. It had a very lovely home feeling and they were accepted quickly and enjoyed evenings with the family before retiring to the guest room, which was actually a detached guest cottage. It was quite nice, they shared a queen bed and when retiring for the night, it was a race to see who got under the mosquito netting last and who had to get the bedroom light on the other side of the room. As usually happens when mother and daughter travel together they would inevitably get the giggles keeping sleep at bay just a little longer.

Day one was from 8am to 3pm spent at Children of Blessings Trust, a center for mothers and children with disabilities run by Kathy Bowler. They bounced along in Kathy's vehicle and turned to avoid pot holes strewn throughout the dirt road, getting to a small local village at a home that housed the projects. It made sense when Kathy told them of placing the program in a local home in an area where the women and children would feel comfortable. The center was comprised of four different rooms according to the child's ability level. The first room was for children that could not sit, the second was for those could sit but could not stand on their own, the third was for preschoolers and the last was for school-aged children.

They wore the local wrap skirts –traditional *Chitinji*- as this was a more remote and traditional area of Malawi and women did not wear pants. It is out of respect to the culture to learn these practices, as one travels. The impact to help others will reach so much further by adhering to cultural norms, (to a certain level, obviously not the unsafe ones).

At the center, each room held "prone-standers" and "activity adaptive chairs" for the children with physical disabilities. Kathy worked together with a few other volunteers to create these chairs and standers that provided cushioning. It took Danell back to her days working in the special education classrooms and hearing of the self-contained classes having to find the budget for a thousand dollar stander or a six hundred dollar specialty chair, whereas here if they need it - they build it and Velcro straps help hold the child in. There was no waiting for the budget to pass or fighting to prove the need. Equipment was just created, if a child needed it they made it, and then they taught the mothers how to use it.

There are not many schools like this here or many places where mental or physical disabilities are accepted. The women carry their children on their back all morning for the multi hour hike to arrive at Children of Blessings Trust for their breakfast and daily therapies where they learn how to support their child with a disability. One woman caught Danell's eye right away as she untied her Chitinji that was wrapped and tied multiple times around her body to hold her eight or nine year-old little boy to her back. His entire body has decided to make simple tasks difficult. His legs were crippled as were his hands. Later Danell met him and learned that he lacked language as well. But what he did not lack was the love of a mother that was rejected by her family because of her choice to continue to raise her child with disabilities. She hiked daily for hours with him strapped to her, knowing that she was receiving services and trying to provide the best life she could for her little man. A mother's drive crosses all cultural boundaries and the strength and determination of mothers worldwide will never cease to amaze on many of Danell's travels; she is continuously awed by them.

They came to do art therapy with the children. Today they worked with upper level students and they would come back later in the week to spend the day doing art with the pre-school children and in the second level classroom. Each trip they learned something new, or realized some need that the Highwire backpacks were lacking in. Every location was very different but with the tools and supplies and seeing how the children react, it gave a good idea of what would be the most beneficial and complete kits globally. There was more overlap in our humanness than many realize and although the geography changes, the human elements are very similar all over the world.

It was on this trip that they learned the importance of not just crayons but having the thick markers as well. One of the kiddos with whom they were doing art therapy was trying so hard, but every time he grabbed a crayon it snapped in two. He had cerebral palsy and crippled hands. Danell reached into their back packs, pulled the cap off the fat-markers, and slowly slid it into his tightly clutched hands! Then they moved the marker over the coloring book together and he began to laugh and smile with such joy that it brought a tear to his mother's eye. The beaming light from mother and child filled the room and quickly spread, as happiness has the beautiful ability to become contagious.

They were to be here all day and took lunch sitting outside, a little mesmerized at all Kathy has accomplished and all the families she teaches and feeds every day. Today was a great day. They were excited at the prospect of returning in a few days to work with another age group.

*   *   *

The next day they planned to join Perry at the Partners in Malawi hospital and complete deliveries to the Thandizo ward. It was a little different kind of delivery than *Threading Hope* was used to doing, as they could not meet those who would cherish the quilts, for reasons of confidentiality. This hospital treated many patients with AIDS and it had a high degree of stigma. The quilts were made to bring comfort and if not meeting the patients helped them feel more at ease, then it was the correct decision. It was also a unique delivery as one quilt does not just go to one person or one family; each quilt will bring joy to many. This ward was a place for very sick AIDS patients to rest and pass. They would utilize these quilts to bring comfort over and over, until they fall apart from washings. The reach of each one will touch the lives of many. What a great place to deliver a little comfort and hope at Partners in Hope.

Perry took them on a tour of the facility and they learned of all the amazing work they were doing, and care they were providing. They were invited to come back the next morning for a ceremony the hospital staff wanted to have for them, to thank *Threading Hope* for the donations.

The celebration was unique as the singing echoed through the halls that were typically- by nature- filled with the sadness of the reality that HIV and AIDS held over this country. The store fronts on the drive to the hospital spoke volumes, a bed maker for new life and cribs, shared a wall with a casket maker who could not keep his shelves filled. After arriving at the hospital they received many handshakes and hugs from the staff and it was a great treat for them to see the staff looking through all the quilts and feeling them and calling over their co-workers with large smiles on their faces. They knew this delivery would do so much good.

They spent the afternoon at Children of Blessing Trust for a lesson of art at the preschool. As they worked with the children Dame;; happened to glance around and her eyes rested at the back table where with her right hand a mother colored with her child at the table, and with her left held her baby for feeding. This very natural scene was beautiful and at the core of our beings as women and mothers. Danell wanted to paint the moment; she found great beauty in it, and an odd feeling of inspiration. The lesson was shorter today and they spent the afternoon coloring in the coloring books and helping the children hold and manipulate the crayons or markers. When they got ready to leave the students met them outside with their *Highwire* backpacks on and were smiling and waving.

Early that evening Brenda took them to the Crisis Nursery, where they met some beautiful babies. They were not here to work, just to volunteer some hug time. They held the babies and did a little pace and bounce technique -and repeat. Although they did not arrive in time to help with the feeding it was a very special place for the Jansen family, as they adopted a daughter from here. It was a neat visit all around, as in Danell's family there are adoptions - an aunt that has adopted children from foreign orphanages and uncles and cousins, so the visit ended up being special for them all. They really enjoyed the evening there, and as the sun settled for the night they felt the fatigue.

The days passed quickly, filled with work and projects. They now could take a breath as deliveries were done, and mother and daughter began to think of what to do with the last days in country. Sleep won out to planning and they drifted deeply into it during conversation.

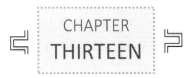

CHAPTER
THIRTEEN

Dog, goat, chicken, pothole...um hyena??

After the humanitarian work concluded they were left with four days...of course they packed in as much as they could. They discussed each other's dreams of Malawi and what each would like to do and figured out a way to combine them. They first looked at safaris and taking a bus from Lilongwe to Liwonde. However, it would cost more for a bus ticket and two nights there, than for them to rent a car, drive to the safari, do a two day package, drive up to Nhkata Bay for some Lake Malawi freshwater diving and back to Lilongwe just in time for the flights home!

That's it, they booked it! Okay drive on the left Danell reminded herself. At the Avis car rental in the Capital Hotel they quickly realized the drive would be an adventure in itself as all cars were manual and despite Danell learning on a manual drive in England at age 14, she had not driven one in well over ten years. That was except ironically, she had a two hour lesson a couple weeks before heading to Malawi to prepare for an interview for a European guide position upon the return to the states and had to drive manual. She had no idea at the time how necessary that mini lesson with her dad would be.

"Don't get me wrong, I think mom would agree, my driving in Malawi was anything but smooth, but we made it and got to do so much more than if we would have just taken a bus!"

It saved money to drive themselves, so another plus, a not so plus… the security stops and pot holes, and animals that lined the roads helped to make it that much more stressful as first gear was always the tricky one. Driving in Malawi became a team sport; mom was co-pilot and helped be Danell's other set of eyes. "Pothole on the left…chicken on the right…person on the left…dog, pothole, goat, pothole…on the left um, big um…what…hyena on the left!"

Soon after the start of their adventure they came to the first security stop, Danell was so nervous her leg would not stop shaking leaving a pushed-in clutch with a little bounce. She was not nervous due to the police being strapped with machine guns - no that was normal, but nervous of the gate and having to talk and start from first gear without stalling and getting the car taken away! Of course she stalled, she tried again…stalled again…looked in the review view mirror and the guard was heading back to her window, she tried again…stalled! She rolled the window down; the guard looked at her for a minute, "What is wrong with this car?" Trying to keep her voice from shaking she said, "It's a rental, must be acting up." Mom tried to keep a straight face as well, but Danell was not sure she remembered to breathe. He stared; she took a deep breath and tried again, Yes!! They were off, that was until the next security point less than 20 minutes away. They must have aged ten years just from the stress, but by the seventh one, it was cake, well, she was not stalling every time at least!

The first adventure planned was our trip from Lilongwe to Liwonde National Park, to the Mvuu camp and lodge. They had approximately a four hour drive on the M1 from Lilongwe to the Hippo View Lodge pick up for a boat transfer.

For the drive to Hippo View they were warned about the possibility of meeting an elephant on the road, "They are usually calm and do not cause trouble but there can be exceptions." Oh wow, team work driving back in action, "*Mom keep your eyes peeled for elephants*," as the words came out of her mouth they both smiled, that was just not an everyday driving rule of thumb. "They show their discomfort or aggression by a swish of the head, flapping of the ears, trumpeting or taking a few deliberate paces towards you; if this occurs calmly and slowly reverse to give them more space." She had a gut feeling that an angry elephant would kind of be easy to spot and the tension would fill the air. Luckily they made it to the parking lot and transfer area angry elephant free, but they were hopeful to see them on our safari!

They were to take a river boat through the Shire River to the Mvuu lodge where they would stay for the next two days for a Wilderness Safari! The 40 km boat ride was a safari in itself, as they spotted hippos galore. Danell loved the ear wiggle they did as their heads gently popped above water and the guttural cough as the boat gets just a little too close.

They arrived to a structured tent hotel room a clever mix of stone and canvas chalet. It was lovely and felt like one was right there with all the wildlife. They had flowers and a beautiful hand written note on the pillows as a welcome, *Zabwino Zonse* (best wishes). The room had canvas walls for tenting and a wooden structure to create a *glamping* experience with flushing toilet and screens on the windows, ahh the simple luxuries, it was fantastic. On the walk to the chalet their paths were crossed by running wild monkeys one of which later that evening was caught by them relieving himself on the front porch, ornery little guy. It was all about location and experience because they can honestly say they both thought it was great, with a little laughter, involved as the monkey left a puddle by the door. Put them back home and a dog doing a tinkle they both would try and scare it away, but no not here, they both watched the monkey with awe and were very quiet as to not disturb his peaceful pee.

Neither are expert bird watchers but they sure could appreciate the beauty of them all through the walking safari and vehicle safari. They were lucky to spot:

African Fish Eagles
Lilians Lovebirds
Grey Heron
Helmeted Guinea Foul
Golden Weaver
Malachite King Fisher
Carmine Bee-Eater
Pied Crow

Blackheaded Heron
House Sparrows
Plum Colored Starling
Pearl Breasted Swallow

It was a fun evening sitting around with the bird books with the guide in the evening to learn all the names of what they had spotted throughout the day. They tried to take notes as they went, but often were mesmerized with the beauty and enormity of wildlife. This is Africa, right? It sure lived up to its reputation; they were having a wildlife-filled adventure.

They signed up for every safari offered -an afternoon boat safari, an afternoon game drive, evening drive safari, and a 5 am early morning walking safari. (Where they hoped to track elephants!!) They were only booked for the one night, two day Mvuu experience and didn't want to miss a thing; they knew they could sleep later.

The afternoon game drive was filled with incredible landscapes, and lush greenery (perk to coming near the end of rainy season). The herds of impala were abundant as were sable, and as the wheels turned they were accompanied by yellow baboons. The wheels on the bus [jeep] continue to go round and round and they found themselves staring at the grandness of kudu and their magnificently curled horns. They got to see the area where the black rhino was protected, *The Sanctuary,* a protected fenced area that also housed zebras. They got to see the striped creature although were not lucky in saying hello to the rhino! Waterbuck and reedbuck were added to the list of African safari sightings, and of course, one must have the warthog; Danell found them very cute!

The evening drive safari took them through the jungle and over to the Shire River where they would get to see the hippos exiting the waters and walking, well more waddling, a little like a rounder Eeyore. The power of each step was felt as it hit the ground and shook the dried grasses they flattened as they walked. Before darkness began to settle in, they got a sunset snack of popcorn and cold drinks as it was quite warm out. The mosquitoes devoured their ankles as they enjoyed the sunset of Malawi surrounded with the echoes of safari and the rhythm of the life, it felt a little like a *Lion King* moment. They were also lucky to have seen the civet and white-tailed mongoose.

The first night *glamping* took a bit to get used to. It was so dark and the chirps and rumbles should lull one to sleep, so what kept them awake. It was the night talks and growls of the hippos-it sounded as if they were right outside the chalet, it sounded like they would just walk right on through the tent. Once they got used to this and felt comfortable enough to sleep, they were off to rest as an early 5am safari awaited the next day. They planned to track the dung of many animals!

Again all about location. If she awakened back home at dawn to go out back and track dung it could be a little odd, but here they were stoked about poop tracking!

They had a hardy breakfast, and cups of coffee before the morning adventure. As they walked to the meeting point they saw huge footprints and were thinking elephant, it was right there inside the camp, fresh prints. When they arrived at our morning meeting spot for dung tracking, the guide gave them an option: "This morning we tracked a herd of elephants that came through our camp, they are close, would you guys like to track elephants this morning? I know it is a change to the program so the entire group would have to agree." The group all excitedly agreed to track elephants. He gave a safety talk and taught some hand signals and snaps to use if anyone saw them, as when tracking elephants one does so in silence and down wind.

They quietly walked, eyes wide open and then "poke" - what ... Danell glanced to her left and there was her mom giving a poke and doing the thigh slap and snap to let the group and leader know she had spotted them!! *Mom spotted the herd; mom caught sight of the wild elephants in Africa and let everyone know.* It was awesome! They began to track elephants for about an hour and got to watch them eat and even spotted a baby. Mind you this entire time they had the leader and the end person that carried the loaded rifle as they tracked. Danell asked with trepidation if it was a tranquilizer; he looked at her as if she were crazy. One would think she would stop here, nope, "*So if we are charged, you will shoot it?*" He nodded his head. "*So when we enter their space, if they are just protecting their own, they get shot.*" He shrugged, and she started to feel a little bad. This was amazing trekking through the jungle on foot tracking elephants in Africa but also just a little disheartening that it could cause the death of an amazing creature. He assured her it was just precaution and he had not had to use it.

It was not five minutes after this conversation that the guide held up his hand in a caution sign, the sign he taught them to take very seriously. Danell looked behind the group and the protection escort had his rifle in the ready position. They all huddled and the guide quietly told them that they had lost track of the mother elephant. She had broken from the herd and fell back. So the majority of the herd was in front of them, but the momma had fallen back to circle around from the rear to protect her baby. "We must be careful and cautious, we are going to head back now, we have gotten too close, stay together and stay quiet as we listen for her movement." Um okay that got the heart pounding! After a bit, they heard the mother in the distance. She had passed them and was catching back up to her herd; now everyone's heart beats must also catch up. Whew that was an awesome experience! One of those experiences that was just amazing because you lived through it. It did not get as crazy as it could have, and to think they could have been cataloging poop, and almost did. There was just that little wrinkle, when the elephant turned the tables and tracked them instead!

The boat safari took them through winding paths within the Shire, and they spotted large lizards in trees, many birds and crocodiles. The boat slowly moved towards the shore where a crocodile was resting. Danell had it perfectly framed in the camera viewing window for a quick video, and as they got closer it snapped its tail and quickly turned back into the water. The sudden movement made her jump. When she jumped, her finger pushed the off button, so instead of a great video she was just in time to catch nothing. They also saw elephants in the distance taking a stroll, as if an internal map guided them gently along the river's edge.

Much of Africa can provide a depth of inner reflection and its landscape can create a look within oneself and a connection that is not expect; it is fascinating that way.

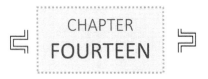

CHAPTER
FOURTEEN

Darwinian Doubt

After a fully-lived last two days filled with animalistic nature and Darwinian doubt, Danell thinks the elephant will always win-out, nose to nose to humanity. *"The need to hold our breath as they searched for a rouge elephant reminded us just how small we really are."* The above ground adventure moved underwater for the next locale, *Aqua Africa*, Nkhata Bay. A little fresh water diving! They arrived in the evening just in time to get some dinner they thought, but the café attached to the hotel was closed and they were about an hour after all the locals had eaten, so *Justin's almond butter* sandwiches from their backpacks it was! They spent the sunset rocking in hammocks by the lake, and as they swung back and forth, they chatted about the trip and then just laid in silence to fully embrace the rising of the moon. It looked full and reflected magnificently across the still waters of the lake.

Lake Malawi is 15,000 square miles and contains more fish than any other lake in the world! It's home to hundreds of species of freshwater tropical fish, many of which can only be found here within the underwater rock formations and caverns, with an amazing array of cichlids specific to this area. Although in a landlocked country this lake mimics oceans with golden sand beaches in the south, and a wonderland 2300 feet deep and well below sea level in the north. The southern end of the lake was crowded and full of bilharzia, a parasite you don't want to catch... so they took to the north as it would lessen chances of getting the parasite. Danell's sights were set on Nkhata Bay. Primarily a port town, which means more local and less touristy- and home to the dolphin fish. Famous for the laid back lifestyle and crystal clear waters, it sounded like an idyllic diving spot. The morning revealed the colors of the sheltered harbor a rainbow of life as the sun glinted across the water and reflected into lush green trees.

Danell's scuba diving was more of a private dive as it was just the instructor and her. Mom went out on the boat with them and enjoyed the ride; she does not dive. There were some great sights, weird too as it was fresh water but the shells and the life were reminiscent of a beautiful salt water dive, one of the reasons Lake Malawi is famous as a diving spot. Danell let out a long slow breath and sank. She then sat with her head in her hands for a good five minutes and watched what looked like a slipper tail lobster make his way in and out of his rocky hole. The famous Dolphin fish swam near and was larger than she imagined and thinner too. Stark silvery gray, with a bit of a pointed face, she could see where it got its name. When the psi had dropped and it was time to slowly rise it was nice to come to the surface and not have the smell of salt water. They went back to the room for a little lunch before departure. They told the guide of their plan but he let them know... "nope, you need more time after completing the dive before you go."

The dive was considered an altitude dive. Danell did not know what that meant until now, so they could not venture back down into the valley for over six hours, they had some time to kill. They looked across the bay and spotted a place that rented kayaks! Danell glanced toward her mother, she was game!   They took off for the 30-minute walk to reach the hostel that rents them. Mind you, Danell's mother is afraid of the water but does not let it beat her, she still takes it on. They asked for life vests, but they were out. They were promised some down by shore but they never arrived. Still mom jumped in the tandem anyway. Clouds were forming and late afternoon approached. They really did not want to drive back to Lilongwe in the dark, as they had been warned not to ever do that. As they curved a land point and could see they were on the opposite side of the bay from the hotel so they needed to paddle their way home! (The kayaks were being picked up that evening at the dock of the hotel, so no need to worry about how to return them) It was great and if they had longer, mom would have stayed out there all day. Danell's only regret with the entire trip was not taking more time on the lake for mom to kayak, as they ended up driving in the dark anyways!

They had a briefing before they left from their hosts in Lilongwe to let them know of the driving rules, 50 km around town 80 km out of town, honk when passing, right blinker on is a sign to not pass, no left on red, if hit or you hit something go to the police – DO NOT stop, and NEVER to drive at night. Man, they were already breaking a rule, and as they drove into the outskirts of the city and got a red light Danell stopped. It was so dark and not a car coming from anywhere. After about twenty seconds she told mom, she was going, it was too dark and deserted. They later found out that one was not supposed to stop at deserted red lights at night as it was where many people get jumped, robbed or other crimes...hum, would have been good to know that one before they left, but they were not to be driving at night so they kind of forgot to ask about night rules.

They made it home excited and exhausted. The darkness of night heightened their senses about a million times more than during the day, as they could not see far in the distance and potholes just jumped out at them. But the best to jump out was the hyena at the edge of the road by the corn fields...only in Africa! They tried to take a photo as they passed but both of their brains where just thinking, WHAT! Neither of their cameras made it out of their bag and add to that, as they slowed the hyena's shoulders reached the roof, they chose not to stop. That and it was right next to corn fields. They had previously been warned of the dangers that lurk inside the fields. Dangers not just for tourists but locals alike - they were made aware that this was a big problem here and it was dealt with daily by the local women.

The morning of their departure from Malawi, Brenda took them to a local market where the stacking of fruit was an art form. Lilongwe is Malawi's capital and the traditional Old Town was still present. It was full of interesting markets and architecture. She took them to the stall where they could buy the traditional wrap Chitinji fabrics; these became part of their memories and their handmade quilts in their homes.

DANELL LYNN

CAPITAL: Quito   Language: Spanish

DONATED to... from Threading HOPE

Colombia

Equator

O Quito

ECUADOR

TRAVEL

Places to be... so much to see...

REPÚBLICA DEL ECUADOR
AIMS MIGRACION AIMS

REPUBLICA DEL ECUADOR
MIGRACION AETO-GUAYAQUIL
NU PASAPORTE: 477055199
16 DIC 2011 02:11
ENTRADA
SALIDA INTERNACIONAL

CHAPTER
FIFTEEN

*South American Adventure, with a Tiny
Stopover in Central America for the
Views of Panama City!*

Landing in Ecuador

The plane was 30 minutes out of Quito, Danell
began organizing her belongings to land, excited
to begin this new adventure and meet fellow
humanitarian Jana Mervine. Just as she put away
her headphones… "This is the captain speaking,
unfortunately there are four planes circling
Quito to land. Fog has closed the airport. We are
unable to circle as we do not have the fuel, and
we are told it will not open for a couple of
hours." They were getting re-routed to
Guayaquil for fuel.

15 minutes went by, and then 30 minutes, the
light drops of rain gave her something to focus
on as they balled and slowly slid down the
airplane window. They sat and sat some more,

she thought they were just here to fuel up but there hadn't been any movement in that direction and the plane just sat in a quiet airport. "This is your captain speaking, we have received word that the Quito airport is still closed and is not going to reopen tonight. Another problem is Guayaquil airport is closing for four hours and this carrier does not have a hub here, so we are working with the locals to try to find hotels and transportation until morning. Thank you for your patience, when we have news we will let you know."

It was well past midnight, and pushing 2 am when they were given yellow cards for boarding of tomorrow's flight. All luggage had to stay on the plane, due to security reasons the luggage door would not be opened. They exited with only what they carried on! The grumbles started and people were concerned with wearing the same clothes for sleeping and for tomorrow. Luckily Danell had all clothes and foods in her carryon as her suitcases below were full of humanitarian donations. She felt relieved for her heavy pack at this time and looked forward to PJ's and snacks.

As they exited the airport they were lined up to load into buses and vans. They were being spread throughout different hotels as not one had last minute rooms for over 100 people. Well, there might have been one but not in the budget the airline was obviously on. Danell ended up on the last bus, and felt as if she may fall asleep standing up. They arrived to budget friendly cockroach infested rooms.

Heavy with exhaustion and worry about how to contact Jana, Danell's body was ready to collapse but she needed to reach Jana. She knew Jana had to take a four hour bus ride from the village to pick her up and now they were in another city completely. At the hotel Victor, a man Danell met on the plane who was in Ecuador to buy his expat home, had a computer. He graciously let her shoot an email to Jana's blackberry about the delay. Danell did not want to start the trip by putting someone out (turns out Jana's friend had an apartment in Quito and she just stayed over after checking and seeing her flight delay). It amazed her the guilt that she could quickly feel if not put in check. The power of worry, if she could only bottle that energy…

One may wonder where was her computer, her blackberry, her smart phone…well yes, she is a world traveler but one that likes to break a little from technology when on the road. She enjoys the disconnection in order to connect and experience other cultures fully. Those are things that she just didn't need (although she was second guessing it at this moment). Danell still believes in going on a trip for a couple weeks without daily contact and most hostels / hotels have computers for guests, so a quick email every couple days is all that is needed to help her friends and family keep their sanity.

As they filtered into the hotel's double doors into a large line - they quickly understood the reason for the delay. Only one attendant was checking everyone in, passport copies, names and pairing people with strangers for roommates! The man in front of Danell was a single traveler also. The last thing she wanted to worry about during this exhaustive humid stay was sharing a room with a stranger of the opposite sex.

Thank goodness a few people in front included a young teacher from Alaska, a woman also traveling solo. This was a blessing in so many ways as the rooms and bedding were quite nasty. The sheets were filled with hair and the flooring and bathroom was decorated with the empty shells of cockroaches. The glass half full moment that could occur with this, at least they were dead!

Her new roomie and Danell got into comfies and pulled out their backpacker towels for top sheets on the bed. They shared snacks as a late-morning dinner and then passed out into the thick exhaust filled air, cherry on top - traffic noise filled room.

They were all told the previous night to be ready for pickup at the hotel at 8am for our flight. They were dressed and ready, filling the waiting room, flowing out onto the curb and lining the walls. 8am turned to 9am turned to 10am turned to 11am and they figured they were forgotten by this time and that the flight had left. One of the young men on the flight had a parent that worked for this airline so he kept everyone informed and on track. Danell, well she always had a book, snacks and although her water was running low, she kicked back and dove right into literature.

Almost 24 hours past the original arrival time, Danell stepped out into Quito. Jana recognized her oversized bright purple duffel that Danell gave as a "spot me" locator. They finally connected after months of emails and a flight delay. It is always gratifying to finally meet the new people you only know via the internet. (Which still amazes her how technology has opened the world unlike anything ever has, it is mind boggling).

Deliveries always look as if Danell were moving into a country with three to four large bags filled with quilts and art supplies and a stuffed backpack. The great thing is it all folds back into itself once deliveries are complete, and she is left with just a back pack. For Paragachi she was bringing 35 hand-made quilts from *Threading Hope* and over 70 backpacks filled with art supplies from *Highwire*. They lugged it all to the buses. A quick buy from the roadside stand of fresh **plantain** chips and up the mountain they went. The bus did not go all the way to Pimampiro. It was a four-hour ride to the end of the line and they were about another fifteen minutes further up the mountain by truck bed. If you went about thirty minutes more you would be in Colombia. As they waited on the side of the road, the overloaded bags made nice chairs while looking out for a ride. In the light sprinkling rain at night on the side of the road in the northern mountains of Ecuador, they got to know each other a little better.

Danell was easily charmed with Jana's warm smile, at first she was quiet, or maybe it was because Danell is quiet, but once talking her light shined brightly. They discussed the home Jana was building that would house a school, classes, volunteers, children in need and so much more. She is a nurse and spends most of her year in Ecuador and then spends a few months stateside to visit family and work to save some funds and then she is back. Entre las Estrellas, Jana sure shines brightly through her foundation, translated – Among the Stars. She dropped Danell off on the cobble stone streets at her hostel which truly was more of a hotel at hostel pricing. She dropped the bags, took a quick shower, and pulled back the sheets to rest; tomorrow the work begins.

CHAPTER
SIXTEEN

Cultural Connections, A Child's Battle,
Art and Accidents

The town **mourned** the loss of a child. A family friend of Jana's had lost their young daughter to cancer just days before Danell arrived. Today holds bitter sweet moments, filled with unique cultural experiences, art classes filled with joy, getting stuck due to road closure, loss of life and more all in a day.

The sweet was heading to Paragachi for a morning meeting with the president of the village, Luis, to discuss the needs and deliveries schedule. The homes were quite spread out so they were creating a game plan for the next day. The bitter was the loss of a child, never something a parent expects, out living one's child feels unnatural to the cycle of life.

North of Quito in the Chota Valley Danell would provide her project services, in a small dusty village where poverty abounds. The first stop

was the home of the village president. When
they arrived, Jana checked Luis' cuts and bruises
to make sure all was healing well. Danell
wondered what had occurred as the scabbed
gash on his leg was a pretty good one. Turned
out youth that had recently found their way to
Paragachi had started a new gang and decided
they did not like the president, as he was trying
to stop the graffiti, so they beat him to show their
claim and distaste.

They met in his home and the president showed
them his bedroom that displayed his true
passion. He was a master weaver, museum
quality, all hand created on his wooden loom.
They sat for a bit and just watched the process;
she was mesmerized. Danell would love a piece
of his work but there were none to buy as he was
in demand and once it was done it sold.

The plans were made so they caught the bus
back to Pimampiro for the funeral. Danell was
invited as a guest. The procession walked the
street to the outskirts of town carrying the
child's casket from the church to the graveyard.
The tombs were stacked above ground about five
high in rows of about ten or twelve. The family
slid the casket in the hole and began to brick it
in, brick by brick with compound in between
each layer. It was as if the sky began to cry the
tears of pain witnessed here. (Often one finds the
world knows when rain is needed to ease the
tears of people.) The showers began, umbrellas

opened and nobody moved. A little rain, a little wet was a small price to pay, and incomparable to the loss of the child. The rain continued to cleanse.

They had scheduled the afternoon for Highwire's art lessons back in Paragachi. Danell headed out alone as Jana had commitments with the family in Pimampiro. She had set up for a local, Sonya, to work with Danell and help with the Spanish for the lessons.

The night before Danell spread the supplies across the bed and created the 71 Highwire backpacks (kits). She does not fill the kits until arrival as it takes up less space for traveling to lay it out as flat as possible. This trip was close to Christmas so it made it a little fun when preparing the kits for classes; the holiday spirit was in the air. She packed up her rolling suitcase with all the filled kits and put her sharpie right on top. She always had one of these to make sure and write each child's name on their backpack. First, so they have claim to it, and second, it gives her a little one on one time with each child as they spell it out to her and they chat.

They arrived at the centrally located one room school house on top of a hill and it was chaos. Children everywhere in and out of the school house, the president and Sonya looked at Danell. They let her know this was how it is, a bit overwhelming. She put the luggage to the front of the room and instructed everyone outside. They would separate into age groups and bring children in 10 at a time for the lesson. She knew once the first lesson was completed and they saw the children with backpacks and supplies they would wait in line. Sonya and el presidente were skeptical, but once they began the first class of 10, in a u-shape with desks and a lesson, smiles grazed everyone's faces. It worked! Danell's many years as an educator in the US helps tremendously in the work she does abroad. The families came in and sat on the benches to the

side as their little ones had an art lesson. There were little hands and eyes trying to peer in the windows, adorable. The windows were high up but they managed to get a peak in. There were lots of laughs and conversations, great art and great connections with the community.

She taught the lessons into the night and even with the light sprinkle of rain the families awaited their turns. It was an amazing lesson and visit. Paragachi had an element of ethereal nature as the clouds hung low and the rain lightly filtered across the hilltop. It was a bit magical.

After the lesson concluded a man came running up to Danell with a young girl, just one and half or two years old. The child's clothes barely fit and were coated with layers of dirt; her nose ran streaming down her lip. Danell looked up and he handed her the child. "Take my daughter," he pushed her to Danell. She looked at him quizzically not understanding what he meant. "We have no more art-kits, our bags are empty, the lessons have finished," she said thinking they did not make it to the schoolhouse. Danell placed her on the ground by her father. "No, no, take her we have too many." Ah, now she understood. The little girl looked up confused at the conversation and Danell's broken Spanish probably did not help but they both understood; she could not take her. As Danell left, as if in self-torture, she looked back. The father had retreated into the gates of their home but the little girl remained, standing in the middle of the dirt road watching them disappear down the hills of the horizon.

When they got to Sonya's house, word had made it back that the big car race had started early, there was no way to get back up the hill. The roads had already closed from the race and they thought they would open soon. Then word came again that there had been a terrible accident and all would be shut down for a while.

At first Danell wondered, should she take off walking into the night back up the hills, as she did not just want to sit for hours at the bus stop. She was not mentally weighing my options for long when Sonya invited her to spend the time in her family home until the roads opened. They walked from the school house down a few hills and over a couple roads, one can think of it like city blocks, down about three streets and over two blocks.

Sonya's home was warm and inviting. They were welcomed by three chickens and a pig that was tied up out front on a rope.

Multiple people lived here, mother, daughters and more. There was one large bed to the left as you entered and two smaller beds separated by curtains. Sonya was maybe in her late 20's; one of the separated bedrooms gave her a little privacy. When Danell first met Sonya's mother she took her hands to Danell's face and just felt it, then she rubbed her arms. Danell is so pale it was fascinating to Sonya's mother. They laughed but Danell could not understand what she said and Sonya translated. She said she wanted her to stay and sleep in the bed with her so she can just look at Danell's pale face.

She ended up being there for many hours and although they never did lie next to each other they connected and Danell just took it all in. The entire experience here was one to remember. She very quickly learned how lucky she was that the road was closed and she got to have this moment with a local family.   Danell ended up being here until close to midnight and throughout the night the mother would sit next to her and just feel her face with a large smile. Her very pale skin was of interest and thus she gave in and even while speaking the mother would reach up and touch her face and she just continued to talk as it if it was normal for someone to continuously rub your face.

Sonya had spent the morning working near a city on the outskirts of the village with the elders. She returned along the mountain trail and gathered a few fruits to share with her family. Tonight as their guest, she insisted Danell have some papaya. She wanted to say no, as there were at least five people living there. But she knew they truly were honored to share it with her, and was honored at their sharing of their home and food with her.

Outside in the detached room they prepared the papaya, in the open air kitchen. A little while later they returned with a plate topped with at least half the papaya for Danell. She began to eat and as they filtered in she shared her plate. They all ate together; with our dirt covered fingers grabbing the fresh fruit. Danell figured if she got a little intestinal bug, it would be completely worth it for this unique in-home moment in another culture.

The mother grabbed her yarns and began to knit a double layer sock-hat for Danell. Danell held the ball of yarn with guidance for correct tension as momma knitted away. They sat next to each other on the bed and quite close. Call it a bubble, a cultural American nature, but Danell scooted just a smidge over for a little personal space, and momma quickly closed the gap. Sitting next to each other leg to leg, putting Danell's bubble to the test, but it felt right so she went with it. The mother took her hand and tapped Danell on the thigh with a "that's my dear" grandma type of pat. So there they sat like two old friends, while momma knitted and measured Danell's head and knitted again.

When she finished a few hours later she had created a puff at the top as large as a hand and with the double layer knit and extra-large puff, Sonya looked up at Danell wearing the hat and started to laugh. Her mother glanced at them both with pride and Danell wore it the entire night, it was lovely, large but lovely. A unique gift from a very memorable time spent with this family in the northern mountains of Ecuador.

After knitting was completed and papayas enjoyed, Sonya asked if she could please paint Danell's nails. She pulled up a stool, took a seat, looked through a selection of colors and armed with baby pink she carefully and gently converted her nails to soft tones of *girl*. Sonya, her mother and Danell sat around and conversed mostly in Spanish. Danell found joy in the sentences she understood and her badly crafted answers, but yet they communicated without barriers. This feeling occurred often for her as her Spanish is far from perfect. While traveling and using my Spanish she held excitement for when it will flow one day, breaking the difficulty languages hold for her!

As night continued to overtake them with sleepy eyes, Jana arrived. The roads had opened. With hugs and another face rub they said goodbyes. Jana and Danell walked down the hills and jumped in the first truck bed they saw and headed north. Danell glanced over at Jana under the glow of lights and she was covered in scratches. She told her the ordeal of the evening and the accident.

The group was all standing on the corner and a semi-truck (no trailer) raced against the cars down the curvy mountain roads. The crowds were excited and the speed and adrenaline filled the air. As the semi took on the curve, the driver went too wide and lost control heading right for the corner where a dozen people stood as on-lookers. Right behind the sidewalk was a little **gulley** filled with rocks and bushes about four or five feet down. As the semi flipped and headed right towards them, they jumped into the gulley. Jana was one of the first to jump and many others landed on top of her. Without a thought of who was down there, people jumped to save their lives as a careening vehicle approached at hyper speed. There was a woman who was sitting on the curb with her infant child in her arms to enjoy the show. As the semi recklessly slid, her motherhood instincts kicked in, and without enough time to stand and jump, before being rolled over, she threw her infant towards a person that caught the child. This mother, instead of clutching tighter, made the ultimate sacrifice and threw her child so it could continue in life as she lost hers. The rolling truck's approach was so fast that there was no time for the mother to stand; it took her life.

As the driver jumped from the truck and began to run, his drunken stupor did not take him far. He was weaving and so slow that it made it easy for the police to catch and arrest him.

It was just day two and major deaths. The child's illness and funeral and now a mother, the village of Pimampiro was heavy with grief.

Selfishly in true human nature, Danell could not help but imagine if the buses were running, she would have been standing there on that corner with her group. She spent the evening becoming culturally rich due to the road closures that may have saved her life. It is interesting how life places you right where you are meant to be. Sometimes it is very clear, like that night, to why she was not meant to make the bus in time.

Busting at the Seams...

Waking up slowly without a rush, the morning dusting of light rain fluttered through the hills. This was her alarm, very different than that which wakes her to work each day back home.

Jana and Danell spent the late morning walking through the local markets. She introduced her to new fruits and vegetables; they had a mini-class on the foods of this area. She was introduced to a lovely mountain fruit called guayabanna. It had a hard shell that covered a soft white lining, filled with a similar texture of the passion fruit, crunchy seeds surrounded with luscious jelly slime...simply divine. It will be year before Danell would have this fruit again - she would have to wait until her visit to neighboring country, Colombia.

They returned to pick up the X-large backpacks and rolling duffle stuffed with quilts, literally busting at the seams. The backpack was so full

Danell was unable to zip it closed and just used its straps to pull it tightly and clip in the quilts. She did her best to fit as many on her back as she could because they would be hiking for miles to deliver these within the village. They arrived around 3pm to meet with El Presidente and Sonya for the hike to the homes of those in deepest need. They would hike through the hills dragging their bags delivering each quilt - one per family. She wished she had a pedometer as their trek took them at least three miles if not four maybe even five. It was 8pm before they finished the last visit and delivery down the hills to a local in high need living on the outskirts.

The very first home they visited, they were invited in. The elder was a man that had lost sight in both his eyes and he wanted them to come in and enjoy a glass of fresh cold juice that his family had made. He was very grateful for the quilt and gave a large thank you hug. It was a wonderful way to kick off our deliveries. He was also the tallest man Danell experienced here. She is 5'7" of average height at home, but here she was tall. Many of the women came up to her shoulders and men just above. She barely noticed it until she got home later and looked through her photographic captures of the trip.

After the first few hours and by their 10th delivery, Luis - El Presidente, began to really get into the spirit. Luis began to announce, "Feliz Navidad – El Presidente," as he knocked on the doors. About an hour later, he added to that with the joy and humor that they all carried, when he announced "Feliz Navidad – Papa Noel!" Families loved it, smiles abounded and this close to Christmas it was perfect that he would be Santa Claus delivering quilts!

The deliveries took them throughout the village from the outskirts to the village center. They planned around the loss of the sun and as evening approached they made our way back to the village center to complete the deliveries. They were met with the sounds of shouts and crying and the police, yet another human tragedy although this time thankfully no one lost their life.

Jana was a nurse so she reacted quickly to assess the needs. Turned out one of the teens in town had illegally given his dirt bike to his younger brother / friend to ride around, yet he was not an experienced rider and did not have control of the bike. He rode with too much speed and lost control taking a turn to wide right into the front yard of a home and running over a young child's thighs. The bike crushed the legs centered perfectly over both thighs. Parents were screaming, children crying, and the police **confiscated** the dirt bike as it was unlicensed so it became their property. The young teen driving was arrested and taken to prison. Even in moments of calm with the deliveries, they were quickly shaken back into the reality of life, and not to take it for granted.

It began to sprinkle lightly as they continued the deliveries into the night setting sky. They walked through the dirt streets and to the right Danell captured a glimpse of an earlier delivery. It was exciting to see it pulling double duty and becoming a jacket in the chilly night air. One of the ladies they delivered to had wrapped herself in the quilt and entered into the life of the evening on the streets of Paragachi. They stopped and got French fries from the road side fryer; Danell passed as they were cooked with chunks of hotdogs, a common staple here.

The reaction of those they delivered to went from extreme happiness, to awe inspired caressing of the quilts. One of the homes they visited had a child that had attended Danell's art class the day before. He ran inside and brought her out a picture he had drawn with a big heart in the center, wishing Danell a merry Christmas and thanking her for all his art supplies. As usually occurred within her when the deliveries and classes finish, on the ride back into Pimampiro, she became quiet and processed the experience. There was so much that was unique about her time here, and the people she met, and the culture. There was a special kind of love here in the northern mountains of Ecuador and its people **radiated** it.

Ecuador with a Side of Panama and Pinch of Peru

Packed and headed for the Quito airport. Jana was heading back to the states for Christmas; Danell was hitting a layover in Panama for the **canals** and then off to Peru to spend Christmas Eve on Machu Picchu and Christmas in Cusco.

When planning her trips and flights, it was crazy that so much money was saved to have a 16-hour layover in Panama and at the perfect time of day for her to grab a cab and head to Mira Flores for a sunset dinner overlooking the Panama Canals. She spent hours there and watched the magnificence as ships went in and out. The size was deceiving until you noticed how small the people were taking control of their duties to make it through the canal.

Down the balcony there was a local family celebrating their daughter's graduation. They stayed many hours as well, and when Danell was trying to take her photos with an outstretched arm the mother asked, "Can I take that for you?" From there they got to chatting, and the mother asked how Danell was getting to her hotel for a short sleep before the flight to Peru. She said she thought to just go down to the street and grab a taxi. The father wondered if she had seen more of Panama and Danell explained that her layover was short so she had planned for the canals and that was about it as it would be night. He said, "You must see more of our city," and they offered her a ride to take a tour of Panama City. She had no hesitation, maybe it was the husband, wife, and three daughters, but it was also the joy that was shared between them and the ex-husband all together with no drama to celebrate the graduation! Danell excitedly said yes and the four girls (3 daughters and Danell) piled into the back seat and squished together for a private evening tour of the city.

It was wonderful! She got to experience old Panama, cathedrals, the history of the three islands built by the United States, the other two canals and the famous Centennial Bridge. Due to his knowledge of his home country and Panama City, one could not ask for a more open experience. As night approached morning they dropped Danell at her hotel for a quick four-hour sleep, then she was off again to the airport headed to Peru.

Peru was an adventure in itself of high altitudes, serendipitous moments, and life changing conversations. Danell arrived in Lima with a day to acclimate and see a little of the city before her flight to Cusco. She met another young solo traveler at the airport and they decided to share a taxi as their hostels were close to each other. They then decided they might as well continue to share a taxi as the both had the afternoon to see the city. La Iglesia de San Francisco had a church and monastery, with the real draw, the underground **catacombs**. From there they enjoyed a walk through the plaza and then back to the hostel for sleeping.

Danell arrived in Cusco a little sick from the altitude and was guided to the dried coca leaves for tea. She made a warm cup and headed to her bunk for some sleep. She continued to drink coca tea every chance she got and it really did help with the altitude sickness. Although the plant is used in creating cocaine, the coca leaf has healthy medicinal properties before turning with the effects of chemical additives. It is not the drug cocaine in leaf form, just a traditional leaf tea. Danell was lucky in that dizziness only stripped a couple of hours from her time here. Many who get altitude sickness become bed-ridden for a couple days to recover. That evening she took a walk to the central part of the city to take in a local dance show at the theater and purchase her tickets for entrance into Machu Picchu.

The next morning her taxi ride to the train station was about twenty-five minutes. When they got there, the driver said that he had no change. Well, that's convenient, the bank only gave big bills and she was not handing that over for the service, so they went into the station to the shops for change. No store had change – really how was that possible, then she heard it... a conversation in English. She walked over to the two gentlemen sitting and asked if they could help her break a bill and make change...they did and saved her. She came back over and sat with them and began to chat. Philip and Wade are two Australians riding their motorbikes from Alaska to Argentina (Circle to Circle). They hit it off right away and chatted for a lot of the four hour train ride into Aguas Calientes. If you ever find yourself needing inspiration for a new adventure the best way is to chat with those out there doing it. Meeting these two would change the direction of Danell's life years later as upon returning from this trip she began to save for a career break and motorbike trip that would lend itself to a minimum of a year on the road, on two wheels, her own solo motorbike adventure. (Blacktie2Blacktop.com)

She treated herself to a stay with Rupawasi for Christmas, a lovely lodge with a vegetarian friendly restaurant up in the trees. After dropping off her bags and changing into her swimsuit she headed to the hot springs. In reality they look very different than what she had in my mind. She envisioned them as natural holes filled with hot springs, the truth was more mini-pools, tiled and perfectly square. She dipped for a bit and then back for a shower and some balcony book reading.

Waking up with dawn on Christmas Eve for her hike up to Machu Picchu. It was drizzling and a little chilly, so she wore leggings and layers, of which she later had to take off on the trail. If you ever feel in shape a way to put yourself in check is a hike at high altitude. She kept doing the stops and looking out into the valley as if it were a planned scenic pause, in reality, she needed air and to just breathe.

When at the top it was exhilarating to look into the sky and literally see the clouds part and the rain stop. Today was also Wade and Philip's planned Machu day, the two gentlemen she had met the day before at the train station. They all hung out and hiked around this massive historical creation. Their personalities were a good match and they laughed and joked throughout the trek. As the day passed and the power from the large rock creations moved over them, it was time to head back down and catch the train back to Cusco. It had not been 10 minutes after they got down from Machu Picchu that the rains began again. It poured the entire train ride out of Aguas Calientes. It was a magical Christmas Eve and she even got to pet a llama on Machu Picchu - that just sounds crazy - pet a llama on Machu Picchu on Christmas Eve!

The next morning her plan was to see the changing of the guard with motorbikes in the Plaza de Armas. She had read about it in a tour book, so she knew the exact time to be ready. Danell headed over, claimed her spot and saw four police bikes change drivers, and thought to herself…was that the changing of the guard? She was about to leave as it was almost an hour past when it was to occur than she saw the cathedral come to life. The doors swung open and people in costume filtered out, dancing and twirling, wearing masks of the most elaborate nature. The colors were bright and beaming, priests carried cradles with a plastic doll inside, and she assumed this was a celebration of Christ's birth for Christmas. So she did not see the changing of the guard, but received a wonderful surprise of celebration instead. Then it was time for the largest market in Peru, a 20 minute taxi ride, and the rain was pouring. Walking through the market many stalls were closed as the rain poured down, and during the downpour she learned her jacket once thought to be rain proof was not, but it was an experience none the less.

Back in Cusco, Wade and Philip invited Danell to join them at the Wild Rover hostel for the large Christmas dinner celebration the hostel was throwing for all travelers in Cusco. There were rows of tables and many seats, and she could not believe how much it felt like the holidays. It was a hostel and they still made this elaborate meal along with table cloths and bows. There was pool playing and dancing; it was a wonderful Christmas celebration and she was glad to have been invited.

Before she left on this trip, she had decided to be more open and let more of the world in. This led to amazing experiences shared with families in the mountains of Ecuador, private family invitations to see the city in Panama, and a connection in Peru that would lead to a decision to take a career break adventure a few years later. From strangers at airports that become a tour buddy for the day, to foreigners finding friendship over creating change for taxi rides, Danell felt more open on this trip than she had been in the past and all because she was willing to experience what life had to give, and so it gave! Trips can change you, and though most are not drastic over time, Danell's travels and trips have helped carve out who she is and this is a large part of her need for it all. The never knowing what may come is exhilarating.

.

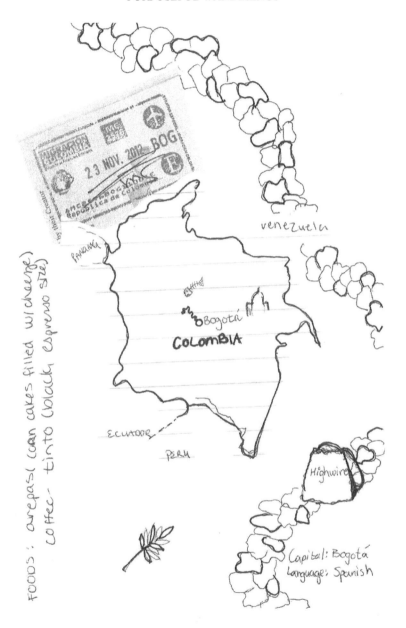

FOODS: arepas (corn cakes filled w/ cheese)
coffee- tinto (black espresso size)

venezuela

PANAMA

Bogotá

COLOMBIA

ECUADOR

PERU

Highwire

Capital: Bogotá
Language: Spanish

143

4:30 am, weighted eyelids, exhaustion slowed the wake-up. The morning was too quick to follow a late night of packing and preparations.

Days Leading to Departure

Combined, Danell's mother and she have been to more than 60 countries, yet the preparation for this trip had looked more like that of a **novice** traveler. Danell forgot to get our malaria pills weeks out so they were stuck with the daily pill instead of her preferred-once weekly, medication. In her drive and preparation from Phoenix to Tucson, she almost forgot her passport. It was hectic and tense as they packed because there were projects to complete at her parent's house. Between the building of an outdoor roof and packing, and doing meals - finally the bags were packed, the roof completed, and they were ready to wake and load the next morning.

They felt as if they were forgetting things but all the important items were packed last weekend. The quilts were bagged and sealed, with all the air sucked out...a dance they have down! Fold, load, vacuum hose...on...off..., twist and tie, tape shut! They can get a lot loaded into just two bags; it is quite impressive. They had all the art kits organized, counted twice and loaded. Filled with excitement and fogginess, it made sense that they felt off and a little lost. It was not many weeks before departure that they lost her father's mother, Edith. Even now Danell can't believe she will never have a sleepover or card games with her again. She was much loved and is much missed. After a long battle with Parkinson's she took her last breath. It was painful and beautiful all in one. Weeks after they lost Edie, and not, but two days before their departure Danell received a call regarding the loss of her cousin. By his own choosing a short life ended at the age of 22. They would miss his funeral while in Colombia, and Danell's dad represented them and conveyed their love to his family. Colombia was a reminder of how precious life is, and her cousin's choice to leave so early only helped drive Danell's need to bring joy to children and families.

Danell had purchased her ticket about a week prior to her mom's purchase, so their outbound US flights and landing in Colombia were together, but the in-between connections were scheduled on different flights. Once they checked in, all seemed good, and they were able to relax; the bags were checked and at the gate – all good!

The flight together to Los Angeles was bumpy and not restful. On arrival in LA, they were sleepy and their bodies were ready for the gate chairs. They had to settle for floor planting, as LAX was crowded with no extra chair space – lucky to find a spot near the wall to lean against. Danell's flight to Miami was a few hours earlier than her mothers, so they hung out at the gate together. They had snacks, chatted and then Danell's flight was called. She had to board, assuming her mom would board the flight an hour later... assuming almost always leads to unexpected outcomes.

Danell arrived in Miami, turned on her phone and had multiple voicemails, and text messages from her mother. She was now in a rush to have her bags pulled from the flight, change her ticket and ahh! It went from a relaxing plan of her getting dinner and meeting her mom at the gate, to chaos. There was not much support from this particular airline, which Danell has yet to ever be impressed with; in all her travels it is never an airline she would recommend.

Her mom's flight "broke" - the main door was leaking fluid, and she was stuck in LA. Then the airline said they could help and change Danell's ticket so they could still fly together to Colombia. Let the chaos continue!

There were arguments between the two agents, the one in LA trying to help Danell's mother and the Miami one telling Danell sorry she should have boarded her flight, mind you these agents both work for the same airline; there was not a changing of carriers. It was time for her mom to catch the next flight to try and get to Miami. So now Danell was in baggage claim with no ticket and no idea if it would work out. Needless to say tears of frustration began to form. No one seemed to care except one woman, Esperanza; she was in baggage claim and was trying to help Danell locate her bags. She was from Colombia and they got to talking about why Danell was heading that way. She tried to locate her bags full of quilts and art kits, but only one could be found, the other was on its way to Bogota. Danell felt defeated and confused, and added to it was worry, as she now had no guidance, no tickets, and was worried about her connecting flight and if she would even get to Colombia. Nothing could be done. It was a "hurry up and wait" situation. So she found a comfortable corner to set herself up with the bag as a foot rest, a quilt as a blanket, and began to focus on relaxing as she waited for her mom's flight. She opened her carry-on for snacks to make a late night meal from tidbits. She could no longer get into where there were restaurants because she was in baggage claim without a ticket.

This entire situation now delayed their entrance into Bogota a full day, so the non-refundable hotel night...well non-refundable. The bigger worry was that the ladies who were to meet them at the hotel would now wonder where they were. So, Danell called her brother in Washington, and gave him some numbers and emails to try and contact for them. Of course, her phone was dying and she could only get a few sentences out before it shut down again.

As was her experience in the past with flight delays, she got a gift, and the woman, Esperanza, was on dinner break. It was close to midnight and she was blessed with a delay to enjoy new company. Esperanza shared part of her dinner with as well as stories of Colombia. They discussed the villages Danell would visit and some meals that she must try! Esperanza was a gentle person with a caring personality that added so much light to the weight the confusion these flights had caused. The world is truly small, what are the odds that on the way to Colombia she would meet a woman from Colombia? They got to chatting about the excitement of *Threading Hope* and *Highwire* and projects around the world. This woman even offered if there were any problems after Danell's mom arrived to call her and she would drive back out and pick them up to stay at her home!

When Danell's mom arrived in Miami, they looked forward to a few hours rest at the hotel that was promised and **vouchered**. They went to stand in line, again. Mom had already stood in line over an hour after landing to get their vouchers and van passes for the hotel. They wait and then got to the front of the line, and the adventure of frustration continued. The van voucher said "one"; they had only listed her mom, even though they both were vouchered for the hotel. The woman said no you cannot ride - you must buy an additional $85.00 ticket. "Are you kidding me," the words so easily flowed out with all the frustrations this airline had dragged them through, Danell could not believe it. They stepped out of line, she told her mom to go on and get rest for a few hours; she would just sleep here in the lobby. The hotel was 45 minutes from the airport and their next flight was in less than six hours. But in true mother's fashion she said, "Let's just go in, find something to eat, and rest at the airport. It would be over 1.5 hours in van rides and then only three hours at the hotel before returning to check in back at the airport." So plan B, they walked around the airport trying to locate a meal after midnight, and end up getting lucky with Subway pizzas. They'd never had that before but it was just what was needed, and they did stay the night in Miami, just not in a hotel!

They found a cold corner in the airport for rest and an outlet to plug in their now dead phones. Each had packed a carry-on quilt that they would later deliver, but for tonight it brought them comfort and warmth. The quilts they each carried were special; Danell's quilt was her first full-designed quilt she had made for *Threading Hope* and the one her mother hand carried was made of fabrics from her grandmother Edith for quilting. They remembered Edie, and curled up to get a few hours of shut eye.

They awakened and both looked puffy eyed and fatigued, definitely not the mixture for winning any beauty pageants. They stretched and felt the aches the cold tiled floors had created. Double checking the status they called her brother, Brandon, for an update and he had gotten a hold of their contact and it was all on schedule to be picked up at the airport in Bogota at 1:30pm upon arrival! It seemed things were starting to align.

So all of this and they had not even reached their destination yet, they had not even left the US...what a crazy adventure so far...Colombia here they come.

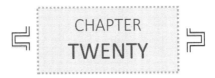

CHAPTER
TWENTY

Mountain curves, Abounding rains,
Broken headlights

The morning after...and a day late...

They finally arrived in Colombia, and were
welcomed in a fashion that felt like a Hollywood
film. After landing and on the way to customs,
they walked up to expansive walls of windows
and could see out into the city and what do they
spot? Full geared police officers with shields and
weapons on one side of the street and protesters
marching towards them right down the middle.
They both looked at each other, smiled,
"Welcome to Bogota."

They walked out of the arrival gate and found the
carts with wheels to help them load bags. It gets
her every time as these are offered for free in so
many countries, but back home in the US, they
charge for this convenience to help with our
luggage. As they loaded their bags in the best

possible way, they did not know at the time that this would become their seat for the next 4 hours!

Their last contact was that Mariana knew about the flight delay and would be there to pick them up...well there was something miscommunicated or something happened...they waited, and waited and walked and waited some more. They walked the entire airport, made a little sign with Mariana's name on it and walked up and down saying, "Mariana, Mariana." Danell had only seen a picture on her Skype profile, so anyone that sort of looked like her probably thought she was crazy as she approached them to ask "Mariana?" They did this for hours, and could not figure out why their contact was not there to meet them. It was going to be dark soon so they had a decision to make. They took the confirmation paper from their folder for the hotel they were supposed to have stayed at last night (even though they lost the reservation). It was the only address in Colombia they had, so they ventured out hopefully to get on to the internet or find a phone and figure out what had occurred and if nothing else find some dinner and a place to sleep.

They got to the hotel front desk, showed them that they were supposed to have been there last night, and asked if they could help and make a call. (The original contact number for a woman in Mexico, Katie Clancy, who is the contact for

Muskoka – Do Good as You Go). The hotel clerk
said yes, and made the call. In talking with Katie
they found out that Mariana and Angela could
not make it to the airport at the time confirmed
with her brother. Katie said she would try and
figure something out and get back to them
through email. They were at the hotel now so
Mariana could find them easily. Danell hung up
as two women were approaching her mom with
bewilderment, "Are you Danell or Kristina?"
Crazy fate, these were the contacts, they just had
a feeling to stop by and see if they were here at
the hotel...then the front desk handed Danell a
bill for the $50 phone call she had just made - did
not see that coming! Guess one should have
asked if the "help us" was free, it was odd as they
already paid for a room they never used, but
such was the case and seemed to be the irony of
this trip so far! "Just hold a hundred dollar bill
out the window and let it fly," said her mom.
Mariana called for a taxi and they were off to the
mountains and to the village about two hours out
of Bogota. They were driving away in the taxi
when Mariana asked Danell if she knew how to
drive, and if women are allowed to drive all the
time. Danell answered yes, thinking that was an
odd question. Then in the Spanish conversation
Mariana was having with Angela, Danell pulled
out some key phrases and looked at her mom.
*"Um, looks like I am about to be volunteered to
drive us out to the village;"* they both nervously
laughed. The last time she drove stick shift was
the craziness in Malawi, and now here they go

again at night on mountain roads, and, of course, it was starting to sprinkle.

The taxi headed to Mariana's Bogota apartment for them to collect her car and then Danell was to drive the mountain roads! Mariana would drive them out of the city but could not drive in the dark in the mountains as she was just learning to drive. Danell and her mother exchanged a glance, another adventure, and she could see her mother's nervousness.

The small drops began to increase and became a full on pouring. Danell was nervous too, as the dark mountain roads had no street lights, no lines, and now it was rain coated. Add to that, the lights on the car did not fully work and fog lined the windows. She drove with the brights on, and realized quickly why Mariana could not see on mountain roads. Her lights did not work properly and you could barely see ten feet if you did not have the brights on. The roads were littered with bumps and potholes, and tree branches. They did not even realize until the next morning how beautiful it was where they were headed as they could not see a thing the night before. They arrived, piled out and her mom said, "You did great!" They both laughed again.

They made it! They had arrived at their destination, rural Colombia, to begin work with Fundacion Construyendo Suenos, working to strengthen families and communities. They were excited but also hungry, tired and had not slept a proper night in days. From airport floors to airline seats, they were ready to reach the rooms and rest. They walked up stairs to their room with two beds, flat style mattresses, and a bath room with a pipe jutting out of the wall for a shower and no toilet seat. Danell found this hilarious and later found pride in how well her mom did! Danell stays in hostels often but this was even further lacking in the basics. They set up their mosquito nets, attempted to shower in the freezing water!

Their home away from home was a residence for elders run by Angela and Senora Aurora, aka "Ma-ma," (a mother-daughter team) that housed those societies had just forgotten about or kicked out. This team of two feed them, helped bathe them, provided therapies, and sang beautifully every night. This was going to be home for the week, and they were fed amazingly, with local food fare and special meals from the area. Every morning "ma-ma" made them fresh café tinto con azúcar. Another favorite was the Agua de Panel warm tea made of sugar cane blocks- it was quite tasty.

The first day was a little chaotic, which was surprising after all those hours of Skype sessions that were to plan the projects day by day. Danell quickly did not see the need for those long conversations as the groups were pulled a bit randomly and decided as they went along anyways. This was often the case and one must shake off the idea of planning and as long as the deliveries get to those that need them and the classes get taught and children get their art supplies, then it is a success.

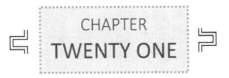

CHAPTER
TWENTY ONE

It takes a village

Sunday

Today was the family unit art lesson. Danell had planned to do the art lesson and then provide the kits, but they found out that they would get a chance for another art lesson teaching the same children in a couple days. So she quickly pulled the markers from the bags to pass around and blank paper so that there would be supplies for the next lesson too.

The family make up in this village varies greatly, from a single mom with three children, a single dad with four children, grandparents raising children alone, and even a grandmother, that was not maternal, but had adopted a little man that had nowhere to go. This woman was raising him all on her own, and making sure he got all he needed-talk about inspirational. Here in San Javier it was true that it takes a village to raise a child and they all work together to make sure that happens.

The art lesson was to help bring the family unit closer together, as well as help them practice public speaking and sharing with the community. Each family member would trace around another family members foot, on the inside they would write / draw what was precious to them and meaningful about their family. On the outside they would discuss what their dreams were for their children and hopes for their family, where they want their feet to carry them. It was a similar lesson to the art lesson from El Salvador done on an individual level, except this one would be about two hours long. After the art work was completed they would present to the group and explain as a family all the things they drew. Many of these stories were powerful and so moving. They were a reminder of how much parents have in common, no matter the country. They all want great success and happiness for their babies.

Danell had brought her translated notes on her lesson directions, so she pulled out a piece of paper and many eyes looked intently at her. Gracias por venir. Vamos a hacer una clase de arte en familia. (Thank you for coming. We will be doing an art lesson as family.)

They all began, whew, it all made sense, a relief. Now she began to walk around and follow up with the basic conversational Spanish skills she had, and was delighted when the right words came to mind to hold a conversation for a few minutes. Language has always been a challenge for Danell and she is excited for the future days that allow a bit of expat living enhancing her ability to become fluent. It makes for funny travel though as she has always had a gift for accents, and often is the case if she knows a few sentences, locals will jump right in to a full-on conversation, and then she must interrupt with apologies and let them know she speaks very little. It never fails that they laugh because her accent sounds "local." It never makes for an awkward situation and usually ends in compliments on her language abilities (which are actually accent ability not language).

The children's art lesson would be on Tuesday, two days from now and they would be doing the families quilt deliveries after the lesson. For today's lesson - the family presentations of their art, they were joined by some other members of the community. Danell and her mother were introduced to a man that has made Colombia his home, Senor Cline. When Mariana told them of his name, she says, "It is like Mr. Clean, the bald cleaner, but Senor Cline not bald."

They sat and chatted over a coffee and tea and quickly found they had lots in common. He invited Danell and her mother to join him and his family at his home the next day for lunch. They were honored, you could see that he had done a lot for this community and was very well respected by the locals. He arranged transportation and the time with our hosts and it was booked for the next day.

After the lessons and presentations it was meal time. Today lunch was taken on the balcony and they watched Senora Aurora hoist the large pot of soup up to the second floor through a pulley system. It was a soup of broth, potatoes, corn on the cob in the soup, avocado, a sour cream like topping, and capers, it is wonderful! They enjoyed a second helping overlooking the rolling hills of Colombia. They also got to enjoy the company of a newly married couple that was honeymooning by riding their motorbikes from California to Argentina. They were just finishing up their photography project through Muskoka in this village as we arrived. It was lovely to chat with Serafina and Aren and to see them off the next morning. Life would re-align them years later soon after their little ones arrived into their budding family.

La Mesa-Monday

The wake-up routine here was quite nice, and the smell of coffee and Arepas cooking made you feel like the old Folgers commercials! They tended to lay and chat in the mornings and not to come down too early, as they were up before much of the house got going. They found that if they came down, Ma-ma felt that she must serve them right away, even though she was busy doing morning routine with all the elders. One morning as they lay stretching in the beds, Danell was pretty sure she woke up the entire house! She did a big stretch, and then there was a huge thud as the boards under her fell out of the bed. It looked like a cartoon as her head and feet were level but my entire midsection sunk down to the floor creating a V shape, and of course, they got the giggles.

This morning Danell tried to convey in her minimal Spanish of the guava, papaya, mango, kiwi, and banana bowl of breakfast that her mom is allergic. It kept coming across that she was sick. It does not help that they both have a continuously running nose, which no was not a cold but a very weird genetic thing! They were always carrying tissue. Along with the fruit they enjoyed coffee and warm Arepas...sooo good.

Today they were headed to La Mesa for the lunch invitation from Senor Cline and his wife Cecelia. He had been a part of this community for years, previously he traveled the world for the film industry. The celebrities he spent weeks with was fascinating and held all the glamour of old Hollywood. He was originally from Holland and his wife is Colombian. Once they found this plot of land, they knew it was where they must live. Their home was beautifully filled with their own paintings and artwork.

They enjoyed hours of conversation over our stir-fried veggies and rice, with a refreshing cup of guayabanna juice. For dessert, warm coffee and exotic fruits, quite nice. They were joined by a pet chickens. They came to you, jump up on your lap and loved their chin scratched!

After lunch Mariana and Angela picked them up and took them into downtown La Mesa, for some sightseeing and a market trip for some needed supplies to enjoy with dinner that night. As they walked the cobble stone streets they were greeted with colorful buildings and laundry lines filled with clothing dancing in the wind. At the edge of the city it opened up to expansive views of the valley, from which they could see the little village of San Javier. Music was playing from a local cantina and Angela grabbed Danell's hands and taught her local moves there in the streets of Colombia, twist here, turn there, hip shake all the time!

Walking back into town for a sweet snack, Danell saw the perfect photo opportunity of a collapsing wall surrounded by a rusting gate, perfect composition. She stepped off the curb and right into it...yes, poop...and not a healthy dog kind, it was runny and gross. She scraped her shoe as she walked across the street to grab a stick and tried to clean out the grooves of her tennis shoes. She sat down and began cleaning so she would not track this into the car. Mariana came over and said "It is ok; it is lucky." At first Danell thought this was a joke, but later when in Bogota, she would again get lucky in Colombia!

They walked to a local street cart for an afternoon snack. It was a flat crispy waffle with caramel sauce, chocolate and cheese with another flat waffle on top. As the years of travel progress, learning to try more of the local food on her trips, although at times for a vegetarian it can be a bit difficult, she still tries as much as she can. As long as the neck bones are removed she could try and fool herself, as she would have to do tonight at dinner, but sometimes it just has to be the emergency almond butter sandwich.

The days felt long, but were passing quickly...it was Tuesday already!

They headed to a village, Pena Negra. They arrived after a long bumpy ride down dirt roads with many U-turns needed, but as said before, "It is all part of the adventure." Today there were six people to the group, an entire family outing with Mariana, Angela, Senora Aurora, Carmen, Danell, and her mother. They arrived with full bladders and in need of cool drinks. Finding a little store front and sat outside to enjoy cold sodas, but Danell had to use the restroom. The young girl running the store showed her out back to the room with a toilet. She looked to her right at the large tree stump that was used as a butcher block, covered in blood and remnants of fat with flies surrounding it. She looked away as chunks rose in her throat, but not before she snapped a photo to show mom later that night. Definitely no eating snacks here!

They headed to the street and walked a few blocks to a school that some of the students they worked with would attend after high school - it was similar to a community college back in the United States. The trees here were amazing and so large. Danell found herself fascinated with the use of bamboo for building. They sat on a bamboo made bench and watched a very bright yellow bird and looked around with disbelief that they had finally made it to Colombia; it was a bit sketchy the first days in the airports, but they were really here.

There were many roaming dogs but different from those seen in many developing countries. They are kept clean and fed; they look like pets but are outdoors all day. It was interesting though that you don't really see female dogs around, almost all are male. Back home we spend four to ten dollars on dog bones. Danell sat in amazement and watched a beautiful boxer enjoy his bone, it looked to be the bottom half of a cow's jaw, for free.

Late afternoon they were in San Javier for the children's art lesson and the family delivery of quilts. They did an art lesson around what they were thankful for and then they shared their amazing pictures. It took some creative language with broken Spanish to try to explain the lesson based on a holiday celebrated back home, Thanksgiving Day. They got it and made really cool "turkey" hand tracings and filled them with what they were thankful for. They were all very grateful for the backpacks, Highwire Mochilas. Estas mochilas estan llenas de regalos de articulos de arte para los niños ... Danell utilized her notes to let the children know the art supplies were a gift and the bags were filled with items to inspire. It was a treat to watch them walk home at the end of the lesson wearing *Highwire* bags and hiking up the cobblestone streets.

They also did the *Threading Hope* deliveries that evening and provided each family with a handmade quilt! It was so much fun to watch them carefully open the folded quilts and inspect all the details and colors! There was another surprise as all the families sat on the steps, arms stretched out with the quilts expanded for an amazing visual and photo!

It's staring at me...the fish...

Wednesday morning was café con leche; most mornings they had café tinto (just a black coffee) with azucar (sugar) for breakfast, fruit and cheese sandwiches. A newish change, as it was one of Danell's favorites when she lived in Miami, Florida. The Cuban style café con leche, and the Colombian are a bit different, both good in their own right. While in Colombia, she preferred café tinto.

Today they went to San Joaquin to get boxes of fresh mangos and see other parts of the surrounding villages. They walked around to the market filled with boxes upon boxes of mangos, but no people to oversee them. The town was actually very quiet with nobody in the streets; it was a bit odd. They walked a couple more blocks to a building that had some boxes outside and were served fresh mangos sliced with a knife that looked like a mini-machete. They were quite tasty and quite sticky as the juices flowed slithering down hands and arms. All were a sticky mess, but luckily there was a wet-wipe in the backpack. Unluckily, there was only one so they all shared attempting to clean the orange stained sticky bodies.

They ventured across a large bridge and saw the smaller part of town filled with village homes. As they stood overlooking the river, in its peacefulness and greenery, Danell looked closer and began to see the full skeletons of cows. They had washed up on shore or died at the edge of the river. None the less, this river supplied the fish eaten by locals, and later that day by them for lunch!

The lunch back at their Colombian home consisted of whole fish and French fries. "He's staring at me," Danell whispered. "Who is staring at you?" mom said, not understanding what the she was talking about as she scanned the room. "No, the fish!" Danell wondered how she would do this. She ate fish sometimes back at home, a few times a year, but it was not still on the bone with skin and eyes that stare up while you rip out its flesh and place it in your mouth. She could not believe it, but she almost ate the entire thing. Some parts she just scooted under the head to look like she had eaten more. It was very hard as all ate together at one table, family style, so she tried not to show that this was difficult for her. Even her mom could not believe how much she ate. She looked around and found humor as all plates but hers were just piled with bones.

Theirs hosts were excited and exclaimed, "This was caught from the river we saw today!" The entire time Danell kept thinking of the dead cows. She was glad that this fish was so hotly fried and hoped it had killed much of what must have accompanied their swim through the waters lined with decaying bones of cows. Whew made it! Washed down with dessert of cheese chunks drizzled with caramel sauce.

The afternoon was one of relaxing. They took their books and fresh tea out to the balcony, and overlooked the lush valley as a light rain fell. They needed a little down time as Danell felt tense. When traveling alone it was so much easier to just go with the flow, she rarely got overwhelmed, but with her mother with her, she wanted it all to go smoothly and perfectly. It was frustrating to her that it was a little chaotic actually doing the classes and the deliveries, which normally was fine, but for some reason she was on edge about it. Danell knew why; she felt responsible for her mother's trip too. So they talked about it, and her mom was having a great time. Danell was all flustered and worried for nothing as she was enjoying it all. This lifted a large weight! Again this had been just an odd trip, you would have thought they never traveled, and for sure never traveled together but this was not the case. Were they just carrying the stressors from back home with them and letting them dictate the trip? On that balcony over tea they let them go, and tried to be more in the present and just enjoy our time together!

Late afternoon they were able to provide the blankets that had been made for this project by elementary students from Denise Green's classroom back in Arizona. The students made hand-tied blankets from fleece. They were delighted to present them to the foundation volunteers who worked so hard at helping everyone else. The volunteers were excited, hugs filled the room! One of the guys, Louis an artist and musician played his guitar. He wrapped himself in his new blanket and they all sat outside and listened to him sing his own songs written about life in Colombia. On their last day he presented Danell with one of his paintings, created on handmade paper from discarded "trash." He mixed it together to create a canvas and then sits on his floor and creates! She has this painting hanging in the living room; it brings in punches of color and happy memories and his songs float back into her mind when she looked at it.

Thursday

This was their last day in San Javier before heading back to Bogota. They had breakfast and enjoyed a quiet morning. They packed their bags and prepared the last delivery of quilts that they would give today to the elders. Many have no family and just a mattress on a frame with no bedding. These quilts will definitely bring warmth and comfort! Each elder was very thankful, and many spouted off quick sentences in Spanish that Danell could not catch, but the grasping of hands, and the hugs said all they needed in order to understand their joy.

They were supposed to leave before 11am as the **exterminators** were coming to spray the village for bugs. They had loaded their bags and were waiting, patiently sipping coffee and journaling, as they heard this horrible noise that sounded like a motor. They glanced up and coming in the front door were two men with "Ghost Buster" style backpacks spraying down the house. They had full gas masks on and glanced up to pause for just a moment at the people sitting in the living room and then continued spraying throughout the home. Angela looked up from her computer but was only deterred for a moment, and then right back to the computer screen! Danell and her mother covered our mouths, "Come on!" Danell shouted. They held their breath and rushed outside!

They did not go back inside and were sitting on the front steps with T-shirts over their faces trying to find fresh air. It was hard to say which was worse, their sweaty arm pits or toxic chemicals. Marianna rushed to them with wet washcloths and told them to put this up to their mouth and nose to help! At this point their throats were burning, eyes were watering and they both looked at each other, "just another part of this adventure." It became the catch phrase for all the weird things that occurred in a matter of nine days since leaving our homes. It was just too funny!

The entire town was getting fumigated. Danell and her mom were ready to leave and when they finally departed, Danell would learn that she was to drive through the mountain again. She really did not want to do so, and said to Marianna, "It will be a good practice day for you as it is daytime, and light out." It worked, she relaxed into the back seat and she and her mom enjoyed the mountainside scenery they had missed when arriving at night. It was beautiful, the Colombia she pictured in her dreams. So lush with rolling hills, donkeys in the fields, sugar cane being harvested, and flower stands filled with poinsettias.

Danell had planned to just arrive and find a hotel, no big deal. Marianna would hear none of it; they booked one in a safe area of Bogota. Danell thought better just go with it, they don't know the area. Excited for a good shower, comfortable bed and relaxing evening. The beds were good, but the loud traffic noise and smog coming through the window they could have done without. They decided to shower before heading to the large supermarket that they had seen driving in. They figured they could get their Thanksgiving meal there! Turned the nobs of the shower, and not freezing, but slow dripping water gurgled out. In an attempt to wash their unwashed hair they used bar soap, as this hotel had no shampoo. It was slimy and dry but at least it was something. They got a little grime off but were far from clean, guess they would shower in two days when they got home!

CHAPTER
TWENTY THREE

A day in Bogota

Breakfast included! A statement often heard by those who stay at hotels. They ventured to the top floor for a warm café tinto and some huevos! They were greeted by silence and an open room with a window for serving. After sitting for a minute they walked to the window to find someone, anyone. Instead they found open tubs of food **swarming** with flies, dirty counters and un-mopped floors. Danell looked at her mom, "Breakfast?" A woman walked in just then, "Tinto?" um, "No thanks." She proceeded to ask if they would like breakfast but they were too busy heading out as they replied, "No gracias." Off to a local café for better luck. They could see a cathedral from upstairs and figured there might be a café nearby. So they hit the pavement.

Today was their only day in Bogota, and they were fine doing the touring on their own, but it was insisted that Mariana and Angela accompany them. Danell felt that it was cultural so they went with it. They were waiting for Marianna to arrive at 10am to go downtown. She showed up but was regretful that she could not stay. She said she would go get Angela and come back with her in a few hours, but then her boyfriend needed the car so we would all just take the bus. Danell looked outside and saw that the bus stop was right out our front door. It was already 10am and they would have to be back by 3pm to check out of the hotel and carry around their luggage for a couple hours before catching a taxi to spend the evening at the airport. They were scheduled to flight out at 1:30am! This left them only until 2pm to enjoy the downtown and the day was passing. Danell said, "It is no big deal, just tell us what stops to take and we will go to the city center for a day of touring." So with regret Mariana gave them big hugs good bye, but they were not deterred. It would be nice to have a day just for the two of them, so they were off and excited to try their hand at public transportation Colombian style! It was actually very easy, straight line there and back.

The city center square was a lot like Trafalgar Square and pigeons were abundant, except here there were also llamas. There stopped first at a pizza to-go place and carried their slices to eat as they walked. They were determined to take it all in. They visited a few churches and even had the time to take in the Museo del Oro of Bogota's history. At record speed, Danell would read off signs as they continued to walk - they got to see so much. Those years of speed reading training really came in handy! It was a great museum and gave them some good information about the country and the areas they had just spent time in.

They carried with them two Highwire kits from their time in the country-side that ended up being extras. Danell brought them into town with them in hopes they might see a child that could benefit. She was glad to have carried them as both found new homes with children sitting street side begging with their parents. The joy on their faces once they realized Danell just wanted to give them a gift, no strings, just fun for their children! One man actually cried he was smiling from ear to ear, as he looked at his wife and his child happily pulling out art supplies from her new backpack! It was a great way to end the deliveries!

They looked around for this year's Christmas ornaments but found no markets that sparked their interest as it was all too touristy. They had found a little shop near the hotel the night before, so they decided to purchase their gifts there later in the day. There is a neat tradition that Danell's parents started when she was a child. The families Christmas ornaments are from places they went to that year; it is a meaningful tradition to Danell and a cool way to bring something small home as a treasure that you pull out once a year in decorating the tree.

They strolled back through the plaza to get to the bus, and she looked at her mom, "Are you sure you don't want to feed the pigeons?" There were many people selling bags of dried corn for less than a quarter, so Danell bought one for each of them. She braved it first and was surrounded; they were on her shoulders, hands, arms, and one jumped to her head and knocked her sunglasses sideways! They were laughing so hard, it was too funny. Danell cut the second bag and poured it into her mom's hands and she was surrounded. She could not pour quickly enough and stepped back for a picture, they were everywhere. It was great fun. The corn was gone, the hours were ticking by and they made their way back to the bus. It was time to check out of their hotel and begin the last leg of the adventure.

During check out, and Danell was completely misunderstanding if she was to pay now, pay twice or pay in a month. Her Spanish was missing some pretty key phrases, so they decided, it is what it is. A slide of the card and they headed out to find dinner with their backs loaded with luggage!

They found a coffee shop, and again had their drink of choice on this trip - café tinto and some bread. Not quite a full meal but a good stop to tide them over until the airport where they would have almond butter sandwiches from their snack bags. They ate so well during the stay that they did not need to eat the emergency meals. There was no use taking it home, so airport dinner was already in their bags.

They checked out, had their bags, bought gifts, got some food and water, and still had some daylight left. They passed a little shop with a hand written sign for manicures. They only cost 2 US dollars - they were in! It was just one little table that overlooked the bustling street. The door was that of a garage and it was partially rolled into the ceiling. It took all they had to not look at each other and laugh as not just their nails but often the entire tip of their fingers got painted.   They got to talking with the owner, the woman painting nails, she let them know that aging was upon her and she could not see very well. They bit their tongues to hold in the laughter not at her vision loss, but as it was quite apparent on their fingers that vision or light might be a factor, but none the less they got a little hand massage, and used up an hour! It was perfect timing to catch their taxi to the airport and be indoors before dark.

They loaded their bags and squeezed into the backseat and as Danell lifted her knees it was here that they saw she had become lucky again. She had dried pigeon poop on my pant leg from the pigeons! They were crying because they were laughing so hard and the taxi driver continued to look quizzically at them in the rear view mirror, "You have fun in Colombia?" he asked. Through her laughter, Danell explained the dog poop and now the pigeon, and he confirmed, "Yes, yes, is lucky!" That was it; they laughed the entire way to the airport!

At the airport they had a bit of Colombian cash to use up so they got a drink, and surprise, it was a coffee. They found a perfect corner, set up their bags, got out their books, and began to make dinner from carry-on snacks! They had to wait as it was only about 7pm and they did not fly out until 1:30am. So the flight number was not even on the boards yet, nor was there anyone from that airline to check in with. They start check in three hours prior, so sat they did, Danell in my bird poop and dirt covered jeans, and mom in her...Danell looked at her mom, "How do you look so clean?" she was baffled! "I brought black jeans, you just can't see it." And they were laughing again.

Colombia was a milestone as *Threading Hope* and *Highwire* both turned five years old, and broke 100 people served and five countries supported, with over 100 quilts delivered and more than 150 children reached by art! It was a magical moment because her mom does not attend all Threading Hope trips, and as the co-founder and her mom, it was very cool for them to share this milestone trip together!

DANELL LYNN

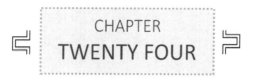

CHAPTER
TWENTY FOUR

Forbidden Lands

There are not many places that have not been explored in today's day and age. The excitement the explorers past felt as they stepped foot on a foreign or unclaimed land, Danell knew she would never feel.

But her heart skipped a beat when she sent her last email confirmation for a trip into Cuba (through the legal channels). Although many nationalities can pass between their homelands and Cuba, for Americans it is not so. And yes, there are "ways" to go, through back channels, but the risk of passport loss was not a risk she could take lightly nor could she ignore. So Danell utilized the legal route on an educator's trip to Cuba. *Highwire* kits were completed and the lesson ideas swarmed in her mind.

There was this element of life that Danell thought was "normal" but the more she aged the more she was proved wrong in her notions of "normal." As she was working on creating this trip for *Highwire* and working the legal angles for entrance, she called her dad and said, "Hey what are your thoughts on Cuba?"

"You mean would I go?"

"Yeah I am working on something that would let us go legally for eight days, because we are all educators. Would you guys be interested?"

There was not a delay; no time spent debating, "Definitely."

"Perfect, I will call you back when ready to book it!"

And thus it began and once the trip moved to a level of approval, mom, dad and Danell sat at the dining room table together and booked their adventure. Two days in Cancun for activities of whale shark snorkeling and Chichén Itzá hiking. Eight days in Cuba and a four day all-inclusive retreat in Rivera Maya to include diving, kayaking, daily ocean swimming, meals without planning, and evening shows. Should be a wondrous adventure!

*   *   *

CUBA

Could you ever imaging that this trip just might start with an airline delay? Their delay in departure would be more nerve-racking if they weren't on a tour. When they heard of the nine-hour delay they just looked at one another, "Hmm" and moved on. Some people were very angry, some cried as they would miss connections and planned adventures. Danell and her family decided to eat.

They arrived at Jose Marti International Airport, bienvenida a La Habana Cuba! Upon exiting the airport, they were met by their guide and bus driver. It appeared that they did not miss much from that first day and were excited to see the city the next morning. This was their first night in Cuba, and at the Presidente Hotel, in Havana. It was just amazing.

The closest to Cuban Culture Danell had the pleasure to enjoy in her past was little Havana in Miami, Florida. She used to love the Cuban coffee shops and fried plantains, true Cuba she was ready to experience!

As dawn broke and after breakfast they headed to the Square of Arms. On top of its impressive history and former colonial buildings, it housed a larger than life rooster. They found out later, as they saw many roosters, that it is a symbol for protection.

It felt good to have the cobble stones under her feet as she walked along such historic avenues. In Danell's true nature she found the pile of dog excrement to fill the empty crevasse of her tennis shoes.

After mild scraping and bonding with fellow tour traveler, Jenny, they laughed wholeheartedly. She had the same experience with a little squishier culprit as Danell did, and this bond would continue throughout the trip.

The group continued on to Cathedral Square and the vast openness surrounded by 18th century colonial baroque architecture, like that of Cathedral of Havana built by the Jesuit order, was simply stunning. The entrance was **captivating** with a red stained wooden double door that became yet another great photo of historic doors to add to Danell's collection of memories. Much of the "old" Havana was under continuous restoration to protect and rebuild the cultural heritage. It was a great undertaking with the weather and salts from the sea, but a very worthy effort. They continued through San Francisco Square and onto to the Children's Theater Company.

They popped in and out of buildings, seeing a little of this and that, including a tiny monastery hostel. But not like what first comes to mind when you hear the word "hostel" or "monastery." It was quite elegant and expensive to match with walls filled of fine art and an open air garden hanging from a cutout in the roof. Her dad sat to rest with a blank face and hands held inner laced on his lap. To his right was a bench mate, a life size copper sculpture of the grim reaper, impressive as the folds in the metal mimic beautifully that of flowing fabric. It easily could have been an eerie photo, but it was captivating instead!

The tours morning plan for the private theater performance became an afternoon show as morning rains delayed the children's arrival. And without the children there it was not La Colmenita Children's Theater. It was well worth the wait, a wonderfully creative and entertaining program. It began as a community art project that has since been given **UNICEF** Goodwill Ambassador Status in 2007 and had charmed audiences from more than 25 countries. The children had amazing talents, and the joyous love story they put on was filled with humor, and audience laughter that depleted every void within the theater. Laughter was so much easier with the adorable and innocent children. They laughed so hard they cried. The talent was apparent, as was the reason of their invitation to perform from New York to Washington to San Francisco.

From little bee costumes to elaborate headdresses, the fashion designer in Danell was in awe. The best was this young little girl of maybe six or seven years of age. She played two different roles throughout the play and was just wonderful to watch. She was very talented, but also very much a six year old. She would be singing then just do a little shake or dance and zone out into her own internal play, loved it. Her twirling and face making added so much that no written screen play could account for!

As they departed it began to sprinkle a light warm rain that accompanied us out of Havana and into the world of Jose Rodriguez Fuster!

*   *   *

Fusterlandia

Take a home, create tiles, shatter plates, add that together and you get the brain child of Cuban artist Jose Rodriguez Fuster.

Welcoming you into the "Village" were walls with Picasso-ish faces tiled to them and fences that line the roads featuring lifescapes. Large roosters garnered the sides of homes, bus stops and benches popped with bright yellows and swimming women, dancing life within the mosaics. Family portraits lined the entrance of his home, each piece carefully placed and not one inch of dullness or plain wall was visible. All was alive within the creations of Fuster.

Upon entering his home, one was greeted with elaborate sculptures and fountains covered in a garden of mosaics- simple and elaborate at the same time- a living contradiction within art and function, captivating. They were invited to his home as private guests to have a tour of his studio and the work space "the wild kingdom of Jose Rodriguez Fuster." They were also treated to a catered lunch at his home, one of the best meals on the entire trip. "Lunch this way," you never need to tell Danell twice that food was on the table. She does love to eat, indulging in the greatness of feeding oneself has never been something with which she ever had an issue. Call it spoiled. She grew up with a mother that could cook, really cook, hamburger helper...what was that, they never ate it! They would travel – her mother would taste it and bring back the creations to the dinner table, truly lucky! Danell enjoy the pleasure of eating, and they were treated during this meal. They had fried fish, black beans, lobster, rice, sliced cabbage (like a coleslaw) fresh fruit, and coke – that purposely took its place on the floor. Ice cold bottled water was what this table needed.

Splashed with tiles and mosaics, highlighted with vintage cars, even from within the bus window as they departed, it was appealing and felt as if in another land.   Fusterlandia was an amazingly visual and creativity inspiring setting that would be wonderful for a children's book. Danell could not help wishing she was riding through this elaborate wonderland without windows or walls, but she knew she would not get her motorbike fixed in Cuba... or would she ... more of her 2-wheeled Cuban ride to come!

Design, Dance and Visual Art

The day continued to the location of an art school.
ISA – Instituto Superior de Arte was the country's
top art academy with programs from music,
modern dance, drama and visual arts. It had
domed roofs and curved brick walk ways leading
to the open courtyard at the heart with a fountain
as a feature sculpture, lily shaped to catch the rains
and run back throughout the drainage. Considered
Cuba's best example of post- Revolutionary
architecture, and was halted and then completed at
a later date.

The genius architecture was created by Cuban
Ricardo Porro and the Italians Roberto Gottardi
and Vittorio Garatti from 1961 to 1965. The site
was green and reminiscent of the mild hills and
rolling greens of a country club, and it was because
during its more affluent heyday it was exactly that.
Havana Country Club golf course, the old
neighborhood Country Club Park was known today

as Cubanacan. Due to the halting of the project the school fell into ruin and in 2001 the Cuban government approached three architects to complete the restoration; it was completed in 2009.

The group visited the print making room and met a few of the students and watched them create their carved stamps and presses. The professor had his work on hand and shared it with them and discussed the process and technique. One of his prints was made from a template creation of layered leaves that he found outside and produced amazing visuals in multiple colors. Andres Dumenigo was the visual artist behind the work that filled the tables. It was great work and visually appealing, and yet Danell was being called to a framed piece on the wall. What had really pulled her in was a black and white ink on paper creation. It was signed Livby or Libby... Danell found herself zoning out in the chaos and focusing into the work for at least three minutes until she felt the eyes of one in the tour group wondering what she was doing. Danell does enjoy solo travel as when she finds herself doing odd things she can just embrace it, no explanation needed; it is divine that way.

They visited areas of painting workshops and some of the group sat outside with complaints. It was easy to walk right by and into what used to be such a revered talent pool. It was only day two and Danell was already aware of those she had no desire to waste conversation within the group nor did she have much respect for them. Sadly it would be proven over and over again, and when adults have childish emotions and actions it makes the psychology background in her begin to analyze. It was analyze or utter frustration in the simple-ness of mind, so instead she chose to look at it as a behavior-learning experiment of sorts.

Today was filled with art and those who create it. The group was invited to the homes and private studios of Juan Moreira and Alicia Leal and viewed current works and the famous works of their past traveling collections. Juan Moreira was the ideal Cuban artist that Danell pictured in her mind with a quality woven hat and white shirt, standing with the wisdom of years and the knowledge of life. They then continued to a warehouse full of artisan and crafts from Cuba for the tourist project of shopping. At times there is way too much touristy stuff in these, but occasionally there are great finds. Danell enjoys her home filled with items from her travels, from the world, not from World Import stores down the street! Later she would add a local-daily use find, which was definitely her preference. It was a local woven market bag. They were walking the streets and she popped in the shop as the group continued and grabbed two, gave over some cash and was back out in less than 30 seconds. A great traditional find - one for her and one for her mom and dad! She loves using these baskets in the home the same way she adores vintage suitcases, adds great practical storage and is a keepsake with practical purpose!

That evening they were treated to some local dance lessons, and fantastic local talent with live music; sweat it up and step to the beats at La Pena del Benny. By the end of the evening they were coated with drenched shirts and no, it was not raining! They were treated to a little more about Santeria; it was here in a backroom covered by a sheet they could get a glimpse into their futures from a Babalawo. Many signed up, and of course there was a fee. Danell went back and forth if she wanted to give it a go. As she talked to the woman who ran the nights introductions and that had been teaching her to dance – the woman grabbed her, gave her a big hug and told her, "You just need to know what you want and go for it, you do not need to pay to be told your future just create it the way you want!" It was the perfect answer to her wondering if she should pause dancing and head back to the quite corner room, it was perfect and she could not be more right on! So they danced on!

*   *   *

Tuesday in Havana

Educational movements have a large part in history, and some enough weight to be dramatically inspiring today. An example was seen through the history of the Literacy Campaign of Cuba. Danell found it uniquely odd that it took travel to Cuba to find educational inspiration that

that she craved. It was ironic because she worked
in state education back in the US.   It made her feel
hope for the illiteracy concerns that plagued much
of the world, that there was a program, a
curriculum that had been developed and written in
Cuba and used in many countries.   She wished it
could come to the US and be used within the prison
systems where illiteracy was rampant, imagine the
positive outcomes!

Luisa Campos, the director of the Literacy Museum,
shared the history as well as the campaigns taking
place in Venezuela, Bolivia, and more, based
around the Cuban campaign model and the
program, *Yes I Can*.

When the campaign began to spread literacy across
Cuba, the call went out and teachers as young as
eleven years old joined and taught those of all ages.
One woman, the oldest to sign up to learn to read,
was in her 90's. In 1961, every Cuban that could
read and write would teach one Cuban that could
not. It was a great success from the revolution and
drastically dropped the illiteracy rate to a number
that was hard to **fathom**, to below 4%, and they
were told it was today less than 2%. Amazing! It
was a pre-education program to learn to read and
write, then one continues by signing up for
schooling and education.
From inspirational movements to preparing those
for higher education, they visited one of the top
Cuban universities, and the oldest, Universidad de
La Habana (Havana University).

During the revolution the stairs filled with students fighting for a new Cuba, and today the stairs continue to serve as the center of student life and social gatherings. Founded by the Dominicans in 1728, the monumental stairway and neoclassical gateways leading to Ignacio Agramonte Square add a history and heartbeat to the educational institution. And all the talks on free education even up through doctorate, made Danell wish she was attending here, the joy of being able to learn without the debt attached, she would have never left school.

Next they would have an afternoon filled with the secondary part to education - the art component. A partial day filled the exotic and very talented creations of Cuban artists that reminded Danell of being in MOMA (Museum of Modern Art). The Museum of Fine Arts Cuban Collection shows the evolution of the last 300 years of Cuban visual arts blending the cultural roots from Spain, France, China, and Africa gave a vast testament to the talent of this island. Firing within a different part of the mind the art spoke but did so quickly due to limited schedules, they were rushed through a few exhibits and missed many others. But their guide was fantastic and spoke fast and walked quickly to make sure they could see as much as possible. Danell was partial and could have spent a full day at least there if not two. The work was amazing and deep, this...art...is her love affair with life, give her a day full of intellect and art...ah mi amor! One of her favorites was the sculptures of the giant cockroach on the wall with a human head. Another

was the extra-large coffee cups filled with
humanlike creatures. It was a bit like walking
through the *Abarat*, a favorite visually stimulating
book of hers by Clive Barker.

Today was long and filled, and their evening was
concluded with a 9pm firing of the cannon at the
Fortress of San Carlos de La Cabana, not just a
tourist affair as the grounds were packed with
locals. Traditionally shot in the morning and the
evening to let Havana's inhabitants know that the
walls protecting the city were opening and letting

merchants know the city was open for trade. In the 19th century it was reduced to one firing at 9pm and has remained since, although today they fire blocks of jute.

Danell remembered being nervous about the tour and making sure that she would get enough packed into her days, as she loves to see all she can in a country with the time that was given to her. Her nerves were pleasantly put at ease in that their guide / tour company made sure they were going from morning until night; it was perfect!

Havana – Bay of Pigs – Cienfuegos
The Bay of Pigs, Maternity Wards, Valley
of Sugar Mills

Visiting the places that are only known from history books holds an appeal. Many of the textbooks are written in the way it is wanted for history to be taught. "True" history, if there is such a thing, takes us on a journey down roads of the past. Danell am not sure that there is a completely "accurate" history book (as no one from that time is alive today), but still she loves reading about it, and learning about events from both sides. For her history is best when you travel to the lands to learn. It is quite fascinating, and to get to place your feet on location is even better.

They left Havana and headed towards Bay of Pigs. They thought they would actually get to see the Bay of Pigs and maybe even walk the ground the historic battle was fought on...that was not the case. Here was a place that that the itinerary was greatly **skewed**, "En route, we will visit Bay of Pigs where the final battle of the Bay of Pigs invasion took place." Where they actually went was a building far from the water that housed the history, the Playa Giron Museum, "featuring the history of the clash and the remains of the invaders armament."

When the group asked if they would get to see the bay of the invasion the tour guide said, "We passed it back there," pointing back down the road from where they had come. It was good that they were not the only ones on the tour that wanted to see this historic landmark, as others also spoke up. They did find out that you could not access exactly where it took place without a hike through the jungle to reach the edge. So they took them to a part of the bay that if they looked back towards the right, they could see the entrance for the invasion, and that was the closest they could get, but that was better than nothing.

They continued to central Cuba making their way to Cienfuegos, "a city of neoclassical buildings with a European flair." There were dropped at the center of the city and visited historical sites around the main square of Jose Marti: the Tomas Terry Theatre 1895, the Casa de la Cultura, the Galeria de Arte Maroya all before check in at the very lovely Jagua Hotel.

The rooms overlooked Cienfuegos Bay and the waters were appealing not just to Danell and her parents but to Jenny as well (Havana buddy through dog feces). She was a swimmer and found the perfect swimming hole to jump into the waters of the bay to start off our mornings. Jenny and Danell's dad would later jump into the waters on the other side of island back in Havana; Danell would be out due to a head and chest cold, but she was ready for the Bay tomorrow!

Day 5 Trinidad

Reading through the plan for the day, "morning: day trip to UNESCO World Heritage Site, Trinidad's Historical Center." Not an everyday agenda one puts into their calendar for the week.

They arrived and were awed again by the extent of care, whether in education or health that was apparent with the visit to the maternity homes – a public health facility. The entrance room was square with a circle of rocking chairs, a very fitting feel, reminiscent of a mother rocking her child to sleep. As they were introduced to the facility Danell found her eyes wandering to the corner where two birds perched in the rafters looking down at the fluttering of rocking.

Any woman with a worry or risk relating to pregnancy was provided care at the Maternity Home. Anything from multiple births, teen pregnancy, pretty much any risk factor and they were provided a place at one of these homes that would care for them. Women were commonly checked into the Maternity Home for additional nutrition and supplements. "Cuba places special emphasis on maternity and infant care, expectant mothers with high-risk pregnancies or other special needs can stay at a maternity home where an on-duty nurse lives and is available 24 hours a day."

As they walked through the facility she found herself still in awe with all that Cuba provides its people for free. These women received shelter, care, food, any needs they had were met. Danell's mind wandered to the homeless pregnant women in Phoenix, Arizona - that are provided dinners and bedding at an evening shelter, but all day care was almost unheard of. And in a city that reaches over 110 degrees Fahrenheit, shelter and nutrition were not available to the extent witnessed today, and especially not free for all women. A program like the Maternity Homes in Cuba would do wonders in many cities she has visited.

*   *   *

Trinidad's historical center and Valley of Sugar Mills were UNESCO World Heritage sites. The colonial architecture and historic essence pulled one further into the past. Homes were filled with luxury antiques and elaborate chandeliers, bringing in elements of old world culture that was an everyday part of life here. At home much of this everyday living would cost thousands to have as your décor, and here in open air homes hung elaborate creations and aging woods. The early days of Spanish colonialism were preserved, not just inside the homes but beyond. The streets exuded history.

Music abounded throughout Cuba, and surrounded by 19th century sugar mills we dined at the Manaca-Iznaga serenaded by the live musical talents of *Manacanabo* -strumming on traditional instruments and playing traditional Cuban songs of this area. As they waited for the meals Danell was bewitched by the sounds and found the perfect little corner to sit and listen. Talk about making a girl blush, the entire band turned to her and played. Her dad laughed, "How does it feel to have your own band?" She thought maybe the band could feel her true enjoyment of their craft; it is hard to capture the Cuban rhythms into words, but it was soul moving and radiates throughout.

After filling our bellies they must climb the historic narrow stairs of the Sugar Mill Tower. They got a bird's eye view of the city and on every level Danell and her mom looked down to dad for their photo op. Danell's dad and heights do not always mix, and this was definitely at the height level that he was good with taking a pass.

On their way back to the bus they picked up some handmade tapestries, an artisan trade specific to the Trinidad area. Ahh, Danell joked, "I am becoming such a grown up, table linens – what's next, 401k's and white picket fences and PTA's. Oh yeah, I have retirement accounts."

When she was not looking she became a grown-up. But oh the older she got the more she gave into the childlike ways of experiencing life, what joy there is in going your own way, cheers to living the life you imagined!
.

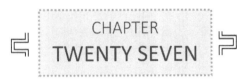

Rhythm of Life
Motorbikes, Revolution & Jazz

By evening they were back in Cienfuegos and preparing for a wonderful evening at a locally owned restaurant for dinner *Finca del Mar – Café and Restaurante.* As they were a family of three they often ended up at a table for four just for the three of them, but tonight they were joined by Alexis their guide.

They had ordered and were awaiting meals when Alexis invited Jeffery (professor from Alaska) and Danell and her mom and dad out to the edge of the bay to sit and chat overlooking the water's edge. They sat looking at the moon's reflection on the water (something that brings enjoyment in any country) and just chatting. It was a nice break from the vastness of group travel and they spoke on anything from the last week, to Cuba, to what they do back home and then a motorbike pulled up. It was the boyfriend of the restaurant owner's daughter. This sparked an entirely new conversation revolving around 2 wheels. Alexis asked Danell if she had ever ridden on one, and when she told him she drives one he did not believe her, a girl driving a motorbike. She told him she rides a 790cc Bonneville back home and he said, "Well yeah, but this one is really big, it is a 250, it is our big bike, very fast."

They were all talking and Danell's dad discussed how they ride as a family and he talked of the trip they did together last summer from Arizona to Colorado, hitting the four corners. Alexis looked at him confused that his family would distance ride. Danell just happen to have one of her magazines, 2 Wheeled Wanderlust (a magazine she founded and writes for). It worked out that she was carrying this for Cuban photo ops because in this issue she had pictures of her riding to show that she actually can and does ride!

The young man went into the restaurant and came back out carrying two helmets (from Honduras). They were awesome helmets that were covered with black leather and the Nike swoosh. She clipped the straps together and they were off – pillion around the streets of Cuba!

When they got back Alexis was saying something to the young man and the next thing she knew, she was tucking her ankle length skirt into the waistband, creating an **impromptu** genie style pants, shifting gears and she was off solo-riding island style!

When she first sat down ready to ride, clutch pulled in, Alexis was nervous and kept explaining to her about the size and how big and fast the bike was and the gears. She could listen no more, so mid-sentence, she was ready and off she went –first to second- second to third, shifting right through the gears riding along the waters of Cienfuegos Bay. The wind blowing through her hair, she knew she had the largest grin from ear to ear as part of her proper riding gear. She embraced the thrill of riding – in CUBA!!

She didn't know the speed limit or the laws for riding in Cuba, it was an impromptu thing, although short and exciting, she headed back to the restaurant after a few blocks.

They went back to the table where dinner sat. A few of the group came out earlier, as the rides began and rudely with a side of jealously stated that dinner was ready. It just did not matter. Danell loved it as even her dad who likes his meals hot, did not even take notice. He and her mom stood as her supporters of the crazy once in a lifetime moment, who cares if the meals were cold, she was going to ride in Cuba! A wondrous moment in time when Danell got to ride a motorbike in Cuba! It was a magical moment. She would not trade it for a warm meal with 17 strangers; it was perfect, serendipity at its finest!

She wrote about the experience for two magazines. It would make the Fall – Winter 2013 issue of *2 Wheeled Wanderlust the Magazine* as a feature story with a photo collage of bikes in Cuba!   It would also have a place in the article for *Mainstream Magazine – Cuba... Ignite your Soul through Culture.* But the best place it would have a feature was in the memory of her time spent in Cuba, a moment that she will not soon forget.

*   *   *

Day 6 -Cienfuegos – Santa Clara – Havana

Morning departure heading back to Havana via Santa Clara, the capital city of the Cuban province Villa Clara. It was here in 1958 that the last battle of the Cuban Revolution occurred, led by **Ernesto Che Guevara**. They visited the impressive Ernesto Che Guevara Square of Revolution and upon departure from the bus it was fitting that today there was a military graduation. Thus the square and the road in front of the **Mausoleum** were filled with young soldiers marching, head to toe green uniforms.

Inside the Mausoleum they quietly entered, removed their hats and pocketed their cameras. The respect for the remains of Che and 16 of his men lay in peace. They were instructed not to speak and the carvings of the men's faces on the placards were haunting with hollow eyes (not in a dark way but in a way that reached deep inside you and camped out for a while). In 1967 they were killed in action in Bolivia, the memorial and crypts were a testament to the legacy Che had left for his people. The square and exhibit featured pictures and memorabilia of the revolution and of Che. Often pictured with his camera in hand or a thick book, he was known not only for his passion but his intellect as well.

It began to sprinkle, just a light drizzle, and within minutes of returning to the hotel a total down pour for the evening. Many of the group were going to a live jazz night at one of the recommended locations on the itinerary. The plan was to walk, but the rain changed that. They were outside the hotel attempting to coordinate taxis but for some reason a couple of people were rushed and didn't seem to care if mom, dad and Danell got separated. Normally they would be fine squeezing into empty seats and spreading throughout multiple cars, but the rush and rudeness from a few of the repetitive – personalities left nothing appealing, added to that the lack of knowledge about where they were actually going. Instead of separating Danell's family decided they would find it on their own.

While they were trying to hail a cab in the rain storm, Benny, from the night of dance lessons walked up with his son! They said big hellos, gave even bigger hugs, and as Eilene walked down for an invited evening with Benny and his son, they all invited Danell and her mom and dad to join them at the best jazz club in Cuba. Another serendipitous moment and perfect timing occurred.

The club within the Cohiba Hotel was Benny's personal club, he owned it! A true jazz club out of the movies from the 1950's. The private tables were pulled together and they sat in as a group enjoying the conversation with the owner. The company was amazing, the live music – Afro-Cuban Jazz at its finest, one could definitely get used to this. And the crazy thing was Benny and his son were going out dancing at an outdoor location, but due to the rains they decided to come here first as the dance clubs were closed. The rains helped to provide Danell's family an awesome night. They felt blessed and so glad they did not squeeze into the other taxis.

Danell tried to fight it, but she could feel a cold was coming on. This was an amazing night but she was ready for the calling of the hotel room and sleep.

Final days in Cuba

Hemingway

Danell had planned to wear her great grandmother's dress for the day at Hemingway's, but the days got changed so she wore it to the day of education and art. Determined today as they headed to Hemingway's she would wear it again and change into it after her art lesson at the community center. She must wear the *Highwire* t-shirt for the community art project, so a cotton skirt for ease of bus seat changing, and nobody even noticed the switch, perfect!!

After breakfast on the final day in Cuba, Danell had waited all week for the opportunity to do the *Highwire* lesson. There were some schedule rearrangements but this was what brought her here. She tried to travel to places where she can also teach and provide art lessons. It was wonderful to meet Pedro Pulido whom she had been in contact with through a third party - you never know quite how that might work out. Having done it now for over five years, she begin each adventure with a deep breath and faith that it would all go great!

The community-based project in Nuevo Vadado neighborhood in Cintio Vitier was a perfect combination of art and community. After a great presentation on the **outreach** work taking place in Colon, and a dance from the children who come here, *Highwire* took the stage. They moved to an outdoor courtyard with round table tops, and some chairs and crates to sit on and for some the tables close enough to the rock wall added seating. It was packed and filled with smiling and laughter. Danell and her parents had backpacks full of art kits and passed out the bags of crayons and notebooks, as she liked to always start with a lesson/project. This time she asked the children to draw for them what they would like to share of their home, what they wanted foreigners to know of their homeland Cuba. The art was creative and powerful, and a few of the students gave their drawings as gifts to Danell which now lovingly fill the walls in her home.

The work that Pedro provides from learning courses for adults to painting, papier-mâché to drama, music to dance and more for elementary and secondary students created a deep support for the community. The passion in his heart radiated and he graciously invited *Highwire* back for a longer project where they could work together for weeks or months at a time on community initiatives with the children. Danell smiled and said with truth that she would love to do so. Although in reality she knew there was a little problem, the **embargo** would make her reentry and extended stay very difficult, but she is hopeful for the day of open passage.

The bus shuffle and change of clothes began in row 3 and by the time they reached Hemingway's villa she was dressed for the occasion.

Danell loves books and enjoys reading and learning. A few years back when she was running her art studio, it became the location of her own book club. When her parents lived in Germany she was in a book club at the local library and would send her dad the books worth reading and they had their own extended book club. During the year in Phoenix that she ran her own, her dad would drive from Tucson for book club night and after it closed they continued their own book club. So it was fitting that for this trip Danell got them Hemingway's, *The Old Man and the Sea*, as they would be where he wrote it!

East of Havana the hilltop villa Finca La Vigia, was where Ernest Hemingway lived from 1939 to 1960. It was here that he created the book club selection! Danell was so excited to visit his home, now a museum, and walk through the halls he did. Sadly they were only able to look through the windows. She was overjoyed to be there and quietly took in the atmosphere that garnered his creative juices that created the works she had ingested for years. Although not allowed to visit it in the way she imagined, it was thrilling to press her face against the old pane windows and see the original books and short story manuscripts. Surrounded by his furniture, priceless art, his fishing tackle, and gun collection were his books; they claimed center stage. With over 9000 volumes filling the shelves and stacked on every available surface.

They contained rare first editions of his works, and works from many other famous writers. The best part her mom pointed out was if you got your nose close enough to the corner of the window you could actually smell the old books! They even got to stand within feet of Hemingway's true love, Pilar, his boat! Danell is very visual and standing here looking at the perfectly stained dark woods, and fishing chairs, created an entire story of pictures in her mind. She envisioned his time floating and casting, letting the lure hit the ocean waves and the rocking of the boat creating a flow of literary words, giving birth to the works read today. She could understand why Cuba appealed to him. As she has said throughout this chapter there was rhythm in Cuba that flowed through you. And as a writer it was easy to see why he made this villa his home!

Las Terraza restaurant opened in 1925 and was Hemingway's hideaway, though not hidden. He frequented it to overlook the river and the fishing boats filtering in and out. Perfectly dressed for lunch in her great grandmother's throw back dress and vintage hat, Danell was ready to do a photo op sitting proper at the corner window that Hemingway wrote from. She sat straight and held a copy of the *Old Man and The Sea.*

You cannot sit at the exact table as it was roped off so she pulled up another chair as close to the ropes as she could get, and it started something. Others in the restaurant began to take the shot as well. It was kind of funny.

The walls were lined with photos of Hemingway, many of which grace the pages of a book she had on Hemingway
and Cuba. It was a wakeful walk through photos and locations she had only read about and seen in her books, a bit surreal.

After their arrival back in Havana, they were given the option to walk Old Havana or visit the revolutionary museum. Danell went to the museum, her mom and dad went walking. They met up later back at the hotel. She was early and had showered and was enjoying a cup of coffee on the terrace when they got in just before the heavy storm hit. They shared each other's photos wishing they had done both, which was actually feasible. Danell visited the previous oval office, gilded furniture and entrances littered with bullet holes from the student movement, and mom and dad got to climb the Bacardi Building tower that over looked the city. They also had time for dad sit with Hemingway at La Floridita. Founded in 1817, this was Hemingway's bar and a life-sized bronze / copper statue of him sat at the bar he had frequented, so her dad got to sit with the bronze Hemingway! They both saw cool things, and all wished they had done both, but did not know until they got back that it was even possible as the museum trip was less than an hour leaving an hour of daylight for exploration. Although Danell did not mind the quiet relaxation of her café con leche and notebook time for writing.

It was their last evening in Havana and even with an upset stomach, Jenny was game for swimming with Danell's dad, so they took off to the Ocean. Her dad had now swam in the surrounding waters of Cuba, the Caribbean Sea and the Atlantic Ocean, pretty cool! She could only claim a Caribbean swim and Atlantic foot dip. With her chest and head cold progressing - jumping from rocks into the ocean and having her head covered in water did not sound like the best choice. It was cool to see the smiles on all the swimmers' faces, Jenny and dad had created a fun little group of swimmers up for the challenge of the Cuban waters. An odd fact the tour guide told them, because he thought it crazy they wanted to swim, was that "most Cubans do not know how to swim." Danell thought he was joking as this was an island, but he was completely serious.

Most trips begin with her humanitarian projects and then a bit of cultural exploration, for Cuba it was opposite and occurred on her last day in Havana before departure. Overall Ishe left Cuba with a guttural desire to stay; there was something there for her, something that felt oddly like home. For a girl who grew up traveling the world and moving often even as an adult, for anywhere to feel a little like home threw her for a loop. She would miss the spirit of Cuba and the vibrant exuberance for life that was apparent in the cities they visited. She saw part of Cuba, not all of Cuba, but what she saw made an impact and she would take away the positive emotions it flared!

CHAPTER
EXTRA

Going into the sixth year of Threading Hope and Highwire Danell headed to Costa Rica. She had two weeks filled with humanitarianism and adventure trips. She was also able to fulfill a dream she had since fifth grade- seeing the sloths in the wild. This "Chapter Extra" is an article she wrote that was published in an adventure travel magazine.

Caution – Read at your own risk...your heart just might melt!

Live Out Loud Philanthropy
By Danell Lynn

There is a special place on the Caribbean coast of Costa Rica. A place where a plot of land gave light to a dream that one couple had in the 1970's. In 1991 a deadly earthquake destroyed the riverboat and bird watching tours they had created. During the rebuild they added a hotel and soon after their dreamed morphed with the delivery of an injured sloth named Buttercup. Little did Judy and Luis know that this little three-fingered bundle would change the direction of the rest of their lives.

It continued to grow and word got around about where to take an injured sloths for rehabilitation. Serving both the Bradypus variegatus - Three-fingered sloth and Choloepus hoffmanni - Two-fingered sloth, this sanctuary has saved lives that would have been otherwise forgotten.

Can a journalist ask for a more serendipitous moment than arriving at the Sloth Sanctuary in Costa Rica with a sloth-in a box-that needs rescuing?

To explain this I will have to go back, way back, to a fifth grade science project. I was that kid...in science club, recycling club, Young Authors, and a track and field athlete...but it was in science class where I wrote my first report on the rainforest. It was here that I fell in the love with the gentle spirit of the sloth and learned of the devastation that was occurring in their natural habitat. Between the Jason Project, Science Club, and the book *Ferngully* by Diane Young, I became a lifelong lover of the rainforest and the species it housed.

When most children's favorite animal was a dog, horse or guinea pig, I longed to one day meet a sloth. It was my favorite animal for more than 20 years before I marveled at three-toed and two-toed sloth's in the wild. And at the Sloth Sanctuary a childhood dream became a reality when I got to meet *Buttercup*!

It was November and I had just spent 5 days at a yoga retreat in the southeastern mountains of Costa Rica. I had only planned this first leg of my trip, everything else I wanted to let the adventure guide me. I did have travel books and had recently read about a woman named Judy and a life of dedication to saving sloths. The day before departure from the yoga retreat I called the Sanctuary to see if they had any of their hotel rooms available for tomorrow night. I was honored that I spoke directly to Judy and booked for the next day. At this time I had seen a few sloths in the wild during my hikes but none up close. I looked forward to learning more about the work she and her belated husband had begun over 20 years ago that has rescued over 500 sloths.

On my day of departure my truck to take me out of the mountains and to my taxi was late. Easy to stay patient in Costa Rica, so I poured another cup of tea and sat in a rocking chair overlooking the treetops and down at the Caribbean. Quiet bliss, then there was a blast charge and the power went out, this happens sometimes so I thought nothing of it, that is until the owner came up to talk with the manager. Then I am told, "looks like you are part of a plan, you will share your taxi." I wondered if he would split the price with me...then half way down the hill the owner jumped out at an electrical pole and loaded sloth into a box – this was my passenger. It was amazing even in the pain of electrocution he looked to be smiling. I stared into the box the entire ride to the Sanctuary and once we arrived the taxi driver help load my arms with my most precious piece of cargo. I walked up the steps to check in and ended up walking in during lunch and Judy knew right away what the box meant. They jumped up ushered me to a table to set him down, I filled out the intake form and then they took him away. Then I just stood there for a moment, Judy said, "thank you." And I said, " your welcome, um...I am Danell we talked yesterday. I am actually a guest staying at your hotel tonight." We all laughed, wow what an entrance.

Humanity has become the hardest part of the sloth's life and due to roads and electrical lines many will come to the sloth recovery shelter in pretty bad shape. Through rehabilitation, research and science the group strives to promote and foster awareness of sloths and educate of their importance to the Costa Rican environment.

Within the sanctuary you can take your pick of the tour to best fit your budget and desire to learn. The *Insider's Tour* will take you behind the scenes into the sloth nursery and the *slothpita*. It includes the "standard" tour but also goes to the specialty spots of infants and incubator babies. There are two times for this tour and they are limited to only 6 people so if you are considering it book early. The other is aptly named *The Buttercup Tour* providing you a one-hour canoe ride where wild sloths will accompany your travel. It is also an introduction to the world of the sloths through natural history and you will get to meet some of the permanent residence that could not be placed back into the wild.

[-tip- if you would like to possibly pet the sloth during the tour (depending on the sloths moods that day) but just in case do not wear any sunscreen or bug spray and you just might get to rub a belly]

For more information or to know how you can help make a difference visit - www.SlothSanctuary.com

AFTERWARD

I hope you have enjoyed this book and have been invigorated in some way to travel, to step out of and see the world-enriching it along the way. Your purchase of this book will help to continue the work of Threading Hope and Highwire, thank you in advance for the lives you have helped enrich.

I hope that these stories and adventures help readers find that they have so much to give, and I hope it inspires many to pack that bag and head out, take to the world one step at a time. "Deciding to travel, deciding to give…" Embrace a life of travel and philanthropy.

Thank you for letting me share my dream of a humanitarian lifestyle, I hope you have laughed, cried tears of joy, and become inspired!

Truly,

Danell Lynn

~Live it to the fullest…this journey of life~

The adventure continues with a yearlong adventure on motorbike. Follow the journey of 1-woman, 1-bike, 1-year, all 50 states and Canada. (www.Blacktie2Blacktop.com)
And yes there will be a book after the journey – tentatively 2016. Keep an eye on the site for exact release dates.

DANELL LYNN

GLOSSARY

Adventure – an exciting or very unusual experience.

Andy Warhol – person - 1928–87, U.S. artist.

Anthropological - the study of the nature and essence of humankind.

Autonomy - the state or condition of having independence or freedom, or of being autonomous; self-government, or the right of self-government:

Bewilderment - a confusing maze or tangle, as of objects or condition.

Bustle - to move or act with a great show of energy.

Canals- an artificial waterway for navigation, irrigation, etc.

Captivating - to attract and hold the attention or interest of, as by beauty or excellence; enchant.

Catacombs - an underground cemetery, especially one consisting of tunnels and rooms with recesses dug out for coffins and tombs.

Chaos - a state of utter confusion or disorder; a total lack of organization or order.

Cobblestone - a naturally rounded stone, larger than a pebble and smaller than a boulder, formerly used in paving.

Confiscated- to seize as forfeited to the public domain; appropriate, by way of penalty, for public use.

Diligently - constant in effort to accomplish something; attentive and persistent in doing anything.

Donations- an act or instance of presenting something as a gift, grant, or contribution.

Embargo - an order of a government prohibiting the movement of merchant ships into or out of its ports.

endearing- tending to make dear or beloved.

Endeavors - to exert oneself to do or effect something; make an effort; strive.

Entrepreneurs - a person who organizes and manages any enterprise, especially a business, usually with considerable initiative and risk.

Ernesto Che Guevara - 1928–67, Cuban revolutionist and political leader, born in Argentina.

Exterminators - a person or business establishment specializing in the elimination of vermin, insects, etc., from a building, apartment, etc., especially by the controlled application of toxic chemicals.

Fathom - to penetrate to the truth of; comprehend; understand.

Foreign- of, pertaining to, or derived from another country or nation; not native.

Gulley - a channel or small valley, esp one cut by heavy rainwater.

Hammam - (in Islamic countries) a communal bathhouse, usually with separate baths for men and women.

Hammock - a hanging bed or couch made of canvas, netted cord, or the like, with cords attached to supports at each end.

Honorable - **1**-in accordance with or characterized by principles of honor; 2 - of high rank, dignity, or distinction; noble, illustrious, or distinguished.

Humanitarian – having concern for or helping to improve the welfare and happiness of people.

Hydroencephalitis – condition where fluids build around the brain.*

Hysterics - a fit of uncontrollable laughter or weeping.

Impromptu - made or done without previous preparation.

Invigorating - to give vigor to; fill with life and energy; energize.

Ironically - pertaining to, of the nature of, exhibiting, or characterized by <u>irony</u> or mockery (Irony - the use of words to convey a meaning that is the opposite of its literal meaning).

Mausoleum- a burial place for the bodies or remains of many individuals, often of a single family, usually in the form of a small building.

Minaret - a lofty, often slender, tower or turret attached to a mosque, surrounded by or furnished with one or more balconies, from which the muezzin calls the people to prayer.

Natural disaster- any event or force of nature that has catastrophic consequences, such as avalanche, earthquake, flood, forest fire, hurricane, lightning, tornado, tsunami, and volcanic eruption.

Novice- a person who is new to the circumstances, work, etc., in which he or she is placed; beginner.

Orphans - a child who has lost both parents through death, or, less commonly, one parent.

Outreach - the act of extending services, benefits, etc., to a wider section of the population, as in community work.

Physiological- consistent with the normal

functioning of an organism.

Plantain- a tropical plant, *Musa paradisiaca,* of the banana family, resembling the banana.

Procession - the act of moving along or <u>proceeding</u> in orderly succession or in a formal and ceremonious manner, as a line of people (*Theology.* the emanation of the Holy Spirit from the Father and later, in the Western Church, from the Son: distinguished from the "generation" of the Son and the "unbegottenness" of the Father.)

⬚adiated- to emit rays, as of light or heat; irradiate.

⬚cholarship - a sum of money or other aid granted to a student, because of merit, need, etc., to pursue his or her studies.

⬚⬚e⬚ ed- to turn aside or swerve; take an oblique course. -to make conform to a specific concept, attitude, or planned result; slant:

⬚tammered - to speak with involuntary breaks and pauses, or with spasmodic repetitions of syllables or sounds.

⬚ustaina⬚le- pertaining to a system that maintains its own viability by using techniques that allow for continual reuse:

⬚⬚ arming - a great number of things or persons, especially in motion.

⬚radition- the handing down of statements,

beliefs, legends, customs, information, etc., from generation to generation, especially by word of mouth or by practice.

⬚nderto⬚ - the seaward, subsurface flow or draft of water from waves breaking on a beach.

⬚NI⬚⬚⬚ - United Nations Children's Fund: an agency, created by the United Nations General Assembly in 1946, concerned with improving the health and nutrition of children and mothers throughout the world; Nobel Peace Prize 1965.

⬚accines - any preparation used as a preventive inoculation to confer immunity against a specific disease, usually employing an innocuous form of the disease agent, as killed or weakened bacteria or viruses, to stimulate antibody production.

⬚olunteer- 1- a person who voluntarily offers himself or herself for a service or undertaking. 2 - a person who performs a service willingly and without pay.

(defs. (n.d.). *Dictionary.com Unabridged*. Retrieved 2014, from Dictionary.com website: http://dictionary.reference.com/browse/defs)

*words not defined from Dictionary.com

Appendix A

Timeline

This timeline covers the beginning of Danell Lynn's businesses and the first five years of trips dedicated to humanitarian ventures.

Here are a few life points not in the timeline that may help to give you a guide of how her achievements and experiences that led to the life she now leads: Danell Lynn was born in 1981, moved often and changed schools every couple years as she grew up in a military family. She attended over 7 schools in her 12 years of schooling and lived in over 12 homes by the time she graduated High School. She started High School in England and then graduated in 2000 in Texas, she received her first degree in Fashion Design in 2002, and her Bachelors in Psychology in 2004 and her Master's in Education in 2010...

󰋞󰋞󰋞󰋞

  -In her mid-20's Danell launched fashion company *dl-couture*, *Danell Lynn Fine Arts* and the humanitarian Company *Highwire*

󰋞󰋞󰋞󰋞

  -First *Highwire* trip to El Salvador
  -Creation of second humanitarian company *Threading Hope*

-Kick off – 1st Quilt for Threading Hope
made for Nata – young El Salvadorian boy
-International Day of Peace – Quilt for the
Parade in Ajo – celebration of peace
around the world

☐☐☐☐
-Threading Hope leads the parade for
International Day of Peace

☐☐☐☐
-July Haiti – *Highwire* and *Threading Hope*
deliveries (first out of country delivery
for Threading Hope – all quilts where made
by Danell's mother and grandmother to
help kick off this journey of philanthropy)

☐☐☐☐
-March –Malawi, Africa -Threading Hope
provided quilts to Partners in Malawi
Hospital and Highwire provided kits and
lessons to Children of Blessing School
-December – Paragachi, Ecuador -Threading
Hope and Highwire deliveries in the
mountains

☐☐☐☐
-Colombia – with the connections of
Muskoka Foundation Threading Hope and
Highwire took their projects into el
Municipio de la Mesa, 2hrs from Bogota

▯▯▯▯
-June – Humanitarian trip to Cuba for
Highwire, was not able to take *Threading
Hope* projects into Cuba due to embargo
-October – first edition of *Philanthropic
Wanderlust* published
-November – Costa Rica (Thanksgiving in
Central America- thankful to give)-
Threading Hope and Highwire took projects
into BriBri villages and schools

▯▯▯▯
-Danell Turned 33 year old
-Young Readers Edition of *Philanthropic
Wanderlust – Purposeful Wanderings*
published

On the weekend of International Day of Peace -
September 2014- Danell Lynn departed for a
year long journey on her motorcycle to all 50
United States and Canada donating a classroom
set (35 books) of *Purposeful Wanderings* to a
school in every state.

www.DanellLynn.com

Appendix B

⬚hreading ⬚ope

⬚

⬚igh⬚ire

Threading Hope

Threading Hope is a Humanitarian entity of dl-couture. It works directly with quilt artists to bring hope to children and those in need in developing areas, providing not just a blanket for warmth but a personalized quilt designed and donated by wonderful quilters around the globe.

Kristina Green is the co-founder of "Threading Hope" with Danell Lynn. Joining together in a lifelong passion of helping others and bringing beauty and hope into times of pain that can feel hopeless.

Are you a quilter, do you know a quilter, want to create and mail your quilts for a good cause? For more information please visit:
www.ThreadingHope.com

Highwire

There has been immense research done looking at the positive effects of art on children. Whether they come from poverty stricken areas, rural communities or even struggling home environments: art has the power to respond in miraculous ways. It builds self-confidence, gives children a voice, promotes thinking skills, and increases cognitive capacities and motivations. Most importantly it reminds them that it is ok to be a child and there are good things in childhood.

The mission of *Highwire* is to bridge the cultural gaps with hope and imagination. Stretching a wire, crossing borders and connecting the human spirit through art!

www.dl-highwire.com

Appendix C

oundationsocations and More

* websites and contacts are assumed accurate at the time of this printing, the internet is a revolving door and may change, the author holds no responsibility to inaccurate / ill-fated links... we did our best to bring you follow up sites to foundations, locations, etc. mentioned throughout this book*

El Salvador

- La Casa de Frieda Restaurant & Hostel – Playa El Zonte
  www.lacasadefrieda.com
- Teresa Rodriguez
  Book – *Daughters of Juarez: A True Story of Serial Murder South of the Border*
  Emmy Award winning Journalist (11 Emmy's)
  Univision News Magazine Show *Aqui y Ahora*
  Twitter: TeresaRodriguez@TereRpdrogiezTV

Morocco

- Teach the Children International
  www.teachthechildreninternational.com
- Center for Women and Democracy – CWD
  www.womenanddemocracy.org
- Fatima Mernissi – author
  www.mernissi.net

Haiti

- MMRC-GLOBAL
  www. mmrcglobal.org

Malawi

- Partners in Malawi (Partners in Hope)
  www. partnersinmalawi.org
- Aqua Africa Dive School and Accommodation
  www.aquaafrica.co.uk
- Mvuu Lodge
  www.mvuulodge.com
- Children of Blessings Trust (Thrive Malawi)
  www. thrivemalawi.ca

⬚cuador⬚

- Entre las Estellas---Among the Stars
  www.amongthestars.org

Peru⬚

- Rupawasi Lodge – Aguas Calientes
  www.rupawasi.net
- Wild Rover Hostel – Cusco
  www.wildroverhostels.com
- Circle to Circle – (Philip & Wade)
  www.bergaliaboys.com

⬚olom⬚ia

- Do Good as You Go (formerly the Muskoka
  Foundation)
  www.dogoodasyougo.org

⬚u⬚a⬚

- Finca del Mar Cefe-Restaurante – Cienfuegos
  (53) 528 24133
- Hotel Jagua –Cienfuegos
  www.gran-caribe.com
- Artist Jose Rodriguez Fuster – Fusterlandia
  www.josefuster.com
- Literacy Campaign
  www.theliteracyproject.org

INTERVIEW EXTRA

Adapted from Arizona State University -Walter Cronkite School of Journalism personality profile by Monica Fidura-Ehlers on Danell Lynn providing light to the giving spirit behind *Philanthropic Wanderlust* and *Purposeful Wanderings.*

Designed to Give

A lot of labels

Sitting in a dim corner of Hob Nobs café, not far from where she lives in downtown Phoenix, Danell Lynn blends with other locals. She sports jeans and a pair of flip-flops, her toenails meticulously painted with dark polish. She wears a simple black wrap sweater and her hair in a messy bun.

It's hard to imagine that a woman who once designed a dress from decks of playing cards could blend in with the rest of us snatching a quick latte or sandwich from the café.

Haute couture in the United States and charity in the Developing World aren't typically synonymous, but for 30-something year old Lynn, no archetypes or abnormalities exist.

All of her endeavors, in detail, would require a short novel at best. Lynn carries about seven separate business cards so people aren't confused or overwhelmed with her various companies and organizations.

Lynn has always had an affection for fine art and giving. Highwire is the first charitable organization she founded to help less fortunate children living in other parts of the world. Through Highwire, she delivers art kits and provides lessons to children in orphanages and hospitals in developing countries. She has just created a coloring book cataloging these adventures that is included in each art kit. Lynn also founded Threading Hope with her mother, which delivers hand-woven quilts to children and families in Developing countries. This book is about these two companies and the global impact being created.

Lynn laughs as she recalls a friend's summary about her life: "You're a vegetarian who rides motorcycles who builds dresses and does humanitarian work in the Third World…what the hell?"

"Labels…I carry a lot of them" Lynn says.

"I was that kid who was in the young author's

club, science club, recycling club, chess club and then a varsity athlete," Lynn says.

Even though Lynn has been exposed to so many different cultures and activities, she grew up with two especially strong influences: art and giving.

Lynn explored almost every school activity, but she always had a preoccupation with the world outside school—especially those who live in a world far different and less comfortable than her own.

Her family took advantage of the opportunities to help in whatever country they lived in or near at the time. When she was about 13 and living in England, Lynn volunteered with her two older brothers and parents to refurbish an orphanage in Estonia. The next summer, Lynn traveled to Kenya to help build homes.

Lynn's inclination to give seemed to start as young as her artistic abilities. Today, Lynn fills her own wallet and empties it, giving away whatever she can at the time. In fact, her fine art and haute couture businesses were built to give back. It should be no surprise that her habits as a little girl grew up with her, defining the way she fashioned her own companies.

Designed to give

Haute couture refers to exclusive, custom-fitted clothing made from expensive, high-end fabrics and sewn with immaculate detail for specific clients.

"It feels more like artwork than just a piece of clothing because you put so much detail into each one and then it's never made again," Lynn says.

She became an apprentice and later assistant designer during her undergraduate work in Florida, working until 3 o'clock in the morning and attending class the next morning as well. Although Lynn was always working and extremely passionate about fashion design, her custom clothing line did not begin until her mid-twenties.

Lynn moved from Florida to Arizona, where her father originally joined the Air Force and has since retired as well. She decided to attend Northern Arizona University for a Bachelor's degree in psychology, another passion she wanted to pursue.

During her time in the psychology program, Lynn met the man she would soon marry and divorce, thrusting her into a different phase of life.

After the divorce, Lynn moved to a small, very affordable artist residence community in Ajo, Arizona, which sits close to the Mexico border. When she moved to Ajo, she declared to herself, "I'm going to find out what I want to do with my life."

Her art and design took a backseat during her marriage. Lynn had done a few shows but had no label on her artwork or fashion designs. "When I got divorced, I really threw myself into it," Lynn says.

During her time in Ajo, Lynn launched *Highwire*. Although Lynn had little money to spare at that time, she put together her first art kit and used buddy passes from airline companies to reach children in South American countries.

"It was just something that came easy to me...through working with children in the Developing World and working with the limited funds I have to make a change." Danell says. "I feel obligated, in a way, to help."

Driven

Back at the café, Lynn taps away on her small

laptop and one of her latest projects sits on the narrow table—a hand-painted clutch made from materials she bought during her trips to other countries, directly from local merchants.

It's the prototype, in a sense, for Lynn's latest charitable business adventure. She is essentially building a business that will fund her other philanthropic investments in Highwire and Threading Hope.

None of her businesses are 501(c)(3) organizations, but they were all built with donating in mind. For instance, dl-couture donates 10 percent of each purchase to humanitarian aid. Humani Handbags is a 50 percent profit share donated right back into Threading Hope and Highwire. And her newly created Cultural Coloring book series donates 100 percent back into humanitarian projects. Lynn also funds her own traveling expenses to countries where she delivers quilts through Threading Hope and art kits from Highwire.

Lynn's saint-like devotion to helping others should not be mistaken for meekness or timidity. On the contrary, Lynn has wielded a shield of perseverance and assertion in the name of her passion.

"Danell, to me, is young," says long-time friend C. Wilson. "She has a lot of the youthful enthusiasm and spirit. And I hope she never loses that. When you've been kicked around as I have, it's nice watching her work with that. She is doing things I wouldn't even attempt to do."

Take for example the 2008 Global Compassion Ball at the United Nations, hosted by Airline Ambassadors International, which provides global humanitarian aid. Lynn dressed Miss America 2008 and Mrs. World 2007-2008. She was the selected designer for the event and her couture dresses were designed to support global programs through AAI.

"All of that takes a lot of patience and a spirit that can't be dampened," says Wilson.

Lynn met Wilson after he purchased one of her paintings about seven years ago and she delivered the piece to his home in California. Wilson, who is in his seventies, has worked with refugees his entire career. Over coffee, Lynn learned of Wilson's refugee work and all they have in common and thus was the beginning to a lifetime of friendship.

"She takes hopeful dreams and turns it into a driven purpose. She has a great perseverance and a high level of intelligence to orchestrate and make things happen," says Wilson.

As Wilson explains, Lynn's attitude is, "Well yea, I did that but let's go out and do something even bigger."

Lynn's own life has taken a unique form like her gowns, but unlike drapery designs, her life cannot be turned into a pattern and fitted for someone else. Her passions, choices, whims, mistakes and successes have created a woman as distinctive as her dresses.

Danell Lynn's memoir lets you leaf through the pages of what feels like her personal journal . The reader gets to witness Lynn's love of humanity, which consumes her heart and her life. Lynn's passion for philanthropy resembles a mother's love for her children—it is the most tender emotion, but also a strong, unrelenting pulse which motivates her to do whatever it takes to reach the needy. Lynn never gives up and keeps on giving, and she convicts us to do the same through the sharing of her journeys across the globe. I will want to share her story with my students in the future, for she epitomizes the manifestation of empathy that we wish for young people to embody as they grow up and lead the world.

Acknowledgements

In life, especial as an artistic introverted writer, it is easy to want to wall inside a cabin and just create...but there are wonderful relationships I would have missed out on.

Thank you to my brother, Brandon, a constant supporter of my writing and being there through many calls to read sections out loud or bounce ideas off of.

For my parents who take on my ventures with open arms and accepting the great differences within me and reminding me to shine.

To my older brother, Jamen, for making sure I have the courage to embrace life and what may come.

Thank you to my friends that upon returning from my many adventures continuously encouraged me to write a book of it all. To my mother Kristina Green, Grandmother Phyllis Eikenberry, and Great-Grandma Mimi Stocksdale, without whom I never would have had quilts to deliver for my first trips, you helped make the dream a reality. To Edith Green who hand sewed labels to quilts even during her fight against Parkinson's, miss you gram. To *Do Good Stitches* and all the quilt circles that have selected Threading Hope as their organization of choice to support through donated handmade quilts, thank you. And to quilter and author Diane Gilleland for the reference to Threading Hope in her book, *Quilting Happiness*, and for the supportive blog story about us.

Thank you to the schools and educators that believe in this book and the hope to help inspire new generations of humanitarians. Truly-thank you!

Lastly, thank you to my best friend Charles who is there for all my many words and concerns with a writer's life, thank you for letting me be my truest self- with no edits -and accepting all that comes with it.

About the Author

Danell Lynn is a globe-trotting writer, international philanthropist, entrepreneur, educator and more. She is the author of *Philanthropic Wanderlust*, *The Parody Series* and a coloring book collection. Her work has appeared in publication from newspapers, magazines, E-zines and books in North and South America. She is the founding editor of *2 Wheeled Wanderlust the Magazine* and former contributing columnist to *Mainstream Magazine*, *Phoenix SportBike Magazine*, and Arts Editor for *The Noise Newspaper*. Her poetry has been featured in *Poetry's Elite*, she was a nominee for the *Governors Arts Awards of Arizona (2011 & 2014)*, recipient of a gratitude award by the First Lady of El Salvador, and has been featured on numerous television and radio programs (Good Morning AZ, FOX 10 Sports News, FOX 10 AZ-AM, CBS 5, KNAU- NPR Radio, NPR-Weekend Edition, Pistol Pete- 92.7 Energy-radio show...).

She lives in the United States, and calls the open road home.
www.DanellLynn.com

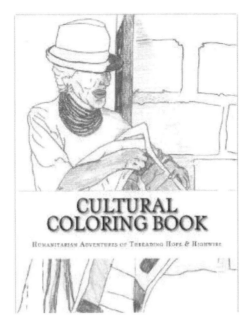

Collect them all… Volume 1 available now.

Explore your artistic nature and embrace your desire to travel and see the world. This first volume of "Humanitarian Adventures of Threading Hope and Highwire" has a collection of sketches for you to bring to life with color.

Travel with us as we deliver quilts and art kits to families and children around the globe. In this first volume we invite you to explore Colombia, Costa Rica, Haiti, Ecuador, Malawi and El Salvador.

100% proceeds of this coloring book go right back into the projects of Threading Hope and Highwire.

Thank you for helping to build cultural awareness
and supporting philanthropic efforts.

Did you love what you read, ways you can help bring philanthropy to many generations.

Write a review:

Goodreads.com

Amazon.com (reviews for print and Kindle editions)

Let all your social networks know about the book, with Facebook, Twitter, email lists and more.

Send an email request to your local library to have it carried in your city for many to enjoy.

Know someone that needs to read this, let them know, or surprise them with a copy as a gift.

-this is a short list please expand your options and help this spread far and wide.

Thank you for your belief in my book, and thank you for spreading Philanthropy!

Truly,

Danell Lynn

Made in the USA
San Bernardino, CA
17 September 2014